# UNDERSTANDING
# DORIS LESSING

## Understanding Contemporary
## British Literature

**Matthew J. Bruccoli,** *Editor*

**Understanding Graham Greene**
by R. H. Miller

**Understanding Doris Lessing**
by Jean Pickering

# UNDERSTANDING
# Doris
# LESSING

by JEAN PICKERING

UNIVERSITY OF SOUTH CAROLINA PRESS

The author wishes to thank the faculty and administrative committees at California State University Fresno who, through a CSU Legislative Award, an Assigned Time for Research Award, and a School of Arts and Humanities Summer Research Grant, enabled her to write this book.

Permission to reprint from a review of *The Good Terrorist* by Jean Pickering. Copyright 1986 by *The Doris Lessing Newsletter*.

Published in Columbia, South Carolina, by the University of South Carolina Press

Manufactured in the United States of America

Library of Congress Cataloging-in-Publication Data

Pickering, Jean.
    Understanding Doris Lessing / by Jean Pickering.
        p. cm. — (Understanding contemporary British literature)
    Includes bibliographical references and index.
    ISBN 0-87249-710-0
    1. Lessing, Doris May, 1919–   —Criticism and interpretation.
    I. Title. II. Series.
    PR6023.E833Z8   1990
    823'.914—dc20                                              90-36183
                                                                      CIP

For B. D.

# CONTENTS

## CONTENTS

# EDITOR'S PREFACE

*Understanding Contemporary British Literature* has been planned as a series of guides or companions for students as well as good nonacademic readers. The editor and publisher perceive a need for these volumes because much of the influential contemporary literature makes special demands. Uninitiated readers encounter difficulty in approaching works that depart from the traditional forms and techniques of prose and poetry. Literature relies on conventions, but the conventions keep evolving; new writers form their own conventions—which in time may become familiar. Put simply, *UCBL* provides instruction in how to read certain contemporary writers—identifying and explicating their material, themes, use of language, point of view, structures, symbolism, and responses to experience.

The word *understanding* in the series title was deliberately chosen. Many willing readers lack an adequate understanding of how contemporary literature works; that is, what the author is attempting to express and the means by which it is conveyed. Although the criticism and analysis in the series have been aimed at a level of general accessibility, these introductory volumes are meant to be applied in conjunction with the works they cover. Thus they do not provide a substitute for the works and authors they introduce, but rather prepare the reader for more profitable literary experiences.

M. J. B.

# UNDERSTANDING
# DORIS LESSING

# CHAPTER ONE

# Career and Overview

## Career

In 1949 Doris Lessing left Southern Rhodesia, now Zimbabwe, for England, taking with her the completed manuscript of her first novel, *The Grass Is Singing* (1950), which, accepted at once by Michael Joseph, the first British publisher she approached, was an immediate success. The following decade, during which she published ten more books, including novels, short stories, autobiography, poetry, and drama, established her as a major British writer.

Doris May Tayler Lessing was born in Kermanshah, Persia, now Iran, in 1919. Her father, Alfred Tayler, a World War One amputee who married his nurse, Emily Maude McVeagh, had emigrated to escape from a postwar Britain he found too confining. His career as a bank official with its concomitant social life centered on British expatriates was as claustrophobic as his existence in class-ridden England had been. Lured by the incentives to immigrate to Rhodesia, recently established as a self-governing British colony, Alfred Tayler moved his family to a new farm a hundred miles from Salisbury. The farm, situated on the edge of the veld, never prospered.

The frontier situation that caused her parents so much distress, however, had compensations for the young Lessing. She often wandered the veld alone, carrying a rifle to shoot game, perhaps a small deer for the family table. This early freedom from the confinements of the female role gave her lifelong independence of mind. The visionary elements in her writing, which shine through even the most realistic of her surfaces, owe much to her father's influence and to her own solitary childhood experiences on the veld. The veld itself is one of Lessing's most enduring images throughout her work—repeated with variations, not all of them necessarily in Africa.

Living on the frontier made her aware of her marginality—the marginality of the observer, a status she has always deliberately maintained, refusing to be co-opted to any group or collective for long. Ironically enough, this marginal status has made her a central figure in contemporary British literature.

Although Lessing was a dedicated reader from childhood, she detested the rigidity of formal education and left school at fourteen, ostensibly because of an eye infection. After two years as an au pair girl in Salisbury, she returned to the farm and began to write. At the same time she was reading extensively, particularly the

## CAREER

great nineteenth-century European novelists such as Balzac, Tolstoi, and Dostoevski and books of contemporary political or social interest such as Hitler's *Mein Kampf* and the sex studies of Havelock Ellis.

In 1938 Lessing left the Tayler farm to work as a telephone operator in Salisbury, the next year marrying Frank Wisdom, a civil servant, the father of her first two children. Three years later she joined a Marxist group and, finding herself unsuited to suburban married life, divorced Wisdom in 1943, the year she published her first poems and short fiction in local journals. In 1945 she married Gottfried Anton Lessing, a German refugee and fellow Marxist, whom she divorced shortly before she left for England in 1949, taking with her Peter, the child of this second marriage.

These experiences form the basis for *Children of Violence*, which she published at intervals over the next twenty years. Although the first volumes of this sequence, which she interrupted to write *Retreat to Innocence* (1956) and *The Golden Notebook* (1962), were well received, it was the publication of *The Golden Notebook* that solidified her reputation and brought her worldwide fame. This novel is still regarded as her greatest work because of the immensity of its conception, its formal intricacy, the inclusivity of its concerns, its historical accuracy, the intellectual capacity of its protagonist, and above all the fact that the entire book asserts that the "filter which is a woman's way of looking at life has the same validity as the filter which is a man's way."[1]

## UNDERSTANDING DORIS LESSING

Lessing's relations with the women's liberation movement have been ambivalent, to the dismay of some of the most fervent admirers of her work. Although *The Golden Notebook* presents the most accurate picture and the best analysis of the situation of women in the 1950s, and though Lessing clearly supports women's rights, she has refused to endorse the movement, seeing its interests as too parochial. Acutely conscious of racism and class divisions, she has consistently seen women's issues in the context of the need for liberation of all oppressed groups.

Until the publication of *The Golden Notebook*, Lessing was regarded as a realist, more precisely a historical materialist. With *The Golden Notebook*, her interest in social reform seemed to have been transmuted into a concern for personal redemption, as Marion Vlastos contends.[2] A rereading of the early novels shows that "Lessing has never truly been the realist (we) critics thought her."[3] She has always been interested in spiritual growth, which is made clear in the later volumes of *Children of Violence*, culminating in *The Four-Gated City* (1969). This novel, developing *The Golden Notebook*'s theme of integration of the personality through madness, ends with a vision of an apocalyptic future; its appendix strikes off in a new direction, which the next three novels—*Briefing for a Descent into Hell* (1971), *The Summer before the Dark* (1973), *The Memoirs of a Survivor* (1974)—and the series *Canopus in Argos* continue.

## CAREER

In retrospect it is clear that the three inner-space novels form a bridge to the outer-space novels. *Canopus in Argos* has provided a context for *Briefing; Summer* is now perceived to be less realistic, and *Memoirs* less prophetic, more hypothetical than at publication. Although some long-time Lessing readers have deplored her venture into space fiction, the *Canopus* series has attracted a new group of readers uninterested in the early realistic novels. To engage their imaginations, which is certainly Lessing's intention in writing this hypothetical fiction, history is defamiliarized by a larger context, one outside contemporary experience of time and space.

Just as she interrupted *Children of Violence*, she set aside *Canopus in Argos* to write *The Diary of a Good Neighbour* (1983) and *If the Old Could . . .* (1984), two novels she published under a pseudonym, now released in a single volume with the title *The Diaries of Jane Somers* under her own name. The concerns of *Canopus*, especially those treated in *The Making of the Representative for Planet 8* (1982), where aging and dying are dealt with from a cosmic perspective, appear as they affect the individual in a realistic context. Since the last *Canopus* novel, *Documents Relating to the Sentimental Agents of the Volyen Empire* (1983), she has written two other realistic novels, *The Good Terrorist* (1985) and *The Fifth Child* (1988), both of which demonstrate her convincing talent for observation of contemporary phenomena.

## UNDERSTANDING DORIS LESSING

### Overview

Doris Lessing has engaged in a lifelong process of self-education, becoming involved with all the important intellectual and political movements of the twentieth century: Freudian and Jungian psychology, Marxism, existentialism, mysticism, sociobiology, and speculative scientific theory. All these interests appear in her fiction, which consequently serves as a record of the changing climate of the times.

Lessing herself resists all attempts to categorize what she has written. She maintains that her themes have remained unchanged since she wrote *The Grass Is Singing* at the very beginning of her career;[4] preferring that her work be looked at as a whole, "she proposes a holistic and, one might say, simultaneous view of her *oeuvre*, resisting any periodization, development, or calculation."[5] It is true that her basic themes have always been present even though the connections between them have not necessarily been obvious from the start. Her ideas have progressed in a way that in retrospect seems inevitable, even though no one could have foreseen that Martha Quest's vision of wholeness represented by the city in the veld would evolve into the Cosmic Harmony of Canopus with its concomitant Necessity. And yet the connections between her basic themes seem always to have been in her mind; she has always been concerned with the larger view, with the problem of wholeness in a fragmentary and compartmentalized world.

At the same time Lessing's novels show a great variety of narrative techniques and forms, including "tragedy, socialist realism, *Bildungsroman,* modernist perspectivism, parody, allegory, quest romance, parable, legend, and science fiction saga," [6] as Betsy Draine points out. Draine further suggests that Lessing's movement from one form to another is, like a pendulum, determined "by the laws of exhaustion and reaction."[7] For example, the tragedy of *The Grass Is Singing* is followed by the mainly comic vision of *Martha Quest,* each constituting a statement about the other in a dialogic interplay. Thus a dialogic development of narrative forms rather than a change in basic themes explains why the surfaces of her narratives are so varied.

Lessing's dialogic impulse also manifests itself in the way in which she reworks these basic themes. She recycles situations: the family circumstances of "To Room Nineteen" are reworked in *The Summer before the Dark* with a different outcome. She reintroduces characters, recalling Martha Quest and Lynda Coldridge from the realistic context of *Children of Violence* to serve in the space fiction of *Shikasta.*

Systems based on opposites have always been attractive to Lessing—the dialectics of Marxism, for example, the juxtaposed conscious/unconscious of Freudian psychology, the Jungian analysis of the psyche as a system of paired opposites, the mysticism and rationalism of the Sufis. But, dating from her earliest years, Lessing's sharp awareness of opposites long pre-existed her interest in political, psychological, and religious systems. The Taylers, living on the frontier on the edge of the veld, were poor by white settler standards, though still immensely wealthy compared to the native farm hands; making her sensitive to inequities of race, class, and gender, this experience of social injustice informs all of Lessing's work. Her mother and father were very different in temperament. Her mother, practical and social, still hoped to return to England when their fortune was made; her father, visionary and solitary, enjoyed above all the expansive view of the veld by day and the stars by night. These oppositions between nature and civilization, between the privileged and the exploited, between the pragmatic and the visionary, have engrained their dialogic pattern on Lessing's world view.

Lessing has drawn a fundamental body of related imagery, appearing in various manifestations throughout her work, from the place where she spent her formative years, the lasting effects of which she details in *Going Home* (1957). The Tayler house of timber, mud, and thatch, built as a temporary dwelling from the materials of the veld, was constantly under siege by ants and vegetation during the twenty years the Taylers lived in it. The house image, together with its inward divisions into rooms and its outward extension into the

city, frequently recurs in Lessing's work, often in juxtaposition with the veld.

Houses of all kinds appear throughout Lessing's
fiction with a range of associations. Sometimes, like the
Turners' shack in *The Grass Is Singing*, the image may
emphasize the fragility of the white settlers' inroad into
the native bush where civilization has a tenuous hold.
Under the influence of the torrential rains—in Lessing's
work dryness and wetness are always gauges of spiritual condition—Mary's final vision shows the house
succumbing to the encroaching bush just as she awaits
a redeeming death. Lessing often uses the house to represent the interior life: Martha Quest, for example, sees
the house of her soul as a half-dozen unconnected
rooms as she waits for a man "to unify her elements . . .
like a roof."[8] Here the image suggests the complexity
of the inner self and the difficulty of integration. The
Coldridge house in Bloomsbury also shelters disparate
personalities, by interacting with whom Martha finally
achieves integration after she has been through new
doors in her psyche because of her "work" with the mad
Lynda in the basement. Kate Brown, dislocated from
the house she has always identified with, manages to
integrate a previously hidden aspect of herself after
spending six weeks meditating in a basement flat. For
these characters, the state of the house represents the
condition of the soul.

Both the house and the city may relate to either the

## UNDERSTANDING DORIS LESSING

public or the private, the individual or the collective: Frederick Karl, for instance, points out that the four houses described *The Four-Gated City* are "microcosms of English society";[9] the Canopean Mathematical Cities in their prelapsarian state are images of both the interior life and the exterior life, for the microcosm and the macrocosm are a single whole. In *The Memoirs of a Survivor* this connection between the city and the house is a structuring principle: the Survivor escapes through the dissolving walls of her apartment from the decaying city where she lives into her spiritual inner space.

There are two versions of the city in Lessing's work, the archetypal city of the imagination, conceived in the Western tradition that includes the Holy City of Jerusalem and the *città felice* of the Italian Renaissance architects, and the twentieth-century metropolis with its impoverished slums, urban blight, and sprawling suburbs.[10] The two are juxtaposed in *The Four-Gated City* when Martha adds a shantytown to Mark's ideal city, underlining the fact that the one makes a satiric comment on the other. Lessing draws attention to the existence of two cities: "Somewhere in our minds there is the idea of a city. A City rather!"[11] The city represents an opposition to nature, suggesting the compartmentalization of the collective mind at its worst; the City in the veld, however, with its gardens and fountains, is a vision of dynamic balance between civilization and nature, between races and generations, the outer and the inner, the macrocosm and the microcosm. It represents

## OVERVIEW

the dream of wholeness, which throughout Lessing's work contrasts with the false wholeness of the collective.[12]

The veld promotes in Martha Quest visionary experiences of oneness with all living forms, adumbrated in the closing scenes of *The Grass Is Singing*. It may be invoked by its absence; for example, in *The Four-Gated City* Martha sees underneath the London pavement the dead clay containing no roots. It can be represented by a single feature such as the tree outside the window of her room in the Coldridge house.

Lessing's juxtapositions of the house, the city, and the veld constitute a many-voiced dialogue accommodating various philosophical concerns expressed throughout her work: the Freudian determinism of *The Grass Is Singing*; the Marxism and Jungian psychology of the early volumes of *Children of Violence*; the Sufism—an ancient form of Islamic human-centered mysticism—of the later volumes and of *Briefing for a Descent into Hell*; and the Laingian antipsychiatry—which holds that schizophrenia, far from requiring conventional psychiatric intervention, is a self-healing illness—of *The Golden Notebook*. All of these theories are applicable to questions of the relationship of the individual to the collective, of identity to role, of civilization to nature.

Whereas individual civilizations—empires—come and go, civilization itself, generally envisioned as a state of being, is regarded as an identifying human characteristic separating humanity from nature. It is only one aspect of the city or the house, each of which has a historical component emphasizing the process of change over time. Those who refuse for whatever reason to recognize change over time—history—are bound for disaster. Alice Mellings of *The Good Terrorist* and Harriet and David Lovatt of *The Fifth Child* all ignore history. Significantly, for all three of them the house is the focus of their desires, which center on a domestic life of a kind invalidated by history. What they do is to ignore necessity, a word that appears in the description of Martha Quest's first visionary experience and is attached to the ideas of biology and history in *A Proper Marriage*.

As her fiction began to dwell less on the conflict between the individual and the oppressive collective and more on the relations between the individual and the whole, Lessing has attempted to deconstruct the opposition between civilization and nature (that is, to demonstrate that this opposition is based on cultural constructs existing in the mind rather than in the structure of the universe) by placing them both in a hypothetical context suggesting potential similarities rather than differences. Such a maneuver is necessary because of the tenacity of this opposition, one promulgated everywhere because of humanity's desire to differentiate itself from brute creation. In its most extreme form, this desire powered the resistance to Darwinian theory. However, Lessing has more than the dignity of humanity in mind; she has been anxious about its survival at

## OVERVIEW

least since 1957, when she wrote "The Small Personal Voice." In *Prisons We Choose to Live Inside* (1987), a series of lectures she gave for the Canadian Broadcasting Corporation, she again articulates her view that the survival of the species depends upon understanding its ties to all creation; thus she considers it crucial that humanity should abandon its sense of separation from nature. To deconstruct the traditional opposition through fictional means, she takes to the larger vision afforded by a view from space.

Lessing's penchant for finding similarity in difference is neatly illustrated by her naming practices. Claire Sprague points out the way in which they call attention to similarities that might otherwise escape notice.[13] Another diarist, Jane Somers, familiarly known as Janna, recalls Anna Wulf, the most famous of Lessing's journal keepers. The mothers of Alice Mellings of *The Good Terrorist* and Harriet Lovatt of *The Fifth Child* are both named Dorothy. Further, Lessing's names imply similarities not only between fictional characters but between fictional characters and people who have played important roles in her life. A witty example is her translation of Frank Wisdom, her first husband, into Douglas Knowell of *Children of Violence*. Her naming Martha Quest's mother May (her own middle name as well as that of her paternal grandmother, Caroline) and giving her mother's own preferred name to Maudie Fowler suggest a stronger link between those two characters than is at first apparent, especially in view of her preface to the *Diaries*, which relates her mother's nature to Janna, with whom Lessing herself specifically disavows any similarity. Martha Quest's daughter, Caroline, bears the same name as Lessing's paternal grandmother. The preponderance of these family names arouses the suspicion that Harriet of *The Fifth Child* may be a sly reference to Lessing's brother Harry. The fact that Emily of *The Memoirs of a Survivor* is named after Lessing's mother echoes her pronouncement that this novel, as the dust jacket proclaims, is "an attempt at autobiography."[14] Her own family constellation appears repeatedly in her fiction, most notably as Mr. and Mrs. Quest of *Children of Violence*. Thus Lessing's novels and short stories are not only self-referential; as the examples noted here indicate, their intertextuality extends to her life as well. It appears that Lessing has deliberately textualized herself as a defense against false division; she believes that a writer's life and writing must form an organic whole: "You have to live in such a way that your writing emerges from it."[15]

As the wide range of her forms suggests, one of Lessing's major preoccupations has been the act of writing itself. She has always taken the profession of writing extremely seriously, citing its demands as a major reason for leaving her first marriage.[16] Her best-known statement on the social responsibility of the writer appears in "The Small Personal Voice": "A writer . . . represents, makes articulate, is continuously and invisibly

## OVERVIEW

fed by, numbers of people who are inarticulate, to whom one belongs, to whom one is responsible."[17] Others appear in introductions and prefaces to novels; her most complex exposition is *The Golden Notebook. The Memoirs of a Survivor, The Marriages Between Zones Three, Four, and Five, The Sirian Experiments,* and *The Diaries of Jane Somers* provide additional commentary. Her latest statement, in *Prisons,* outlines her belief that the writer's prime responsibility is a social one, explaining that a novelist's most valuable contribution is "to enable us to see ourselves as others see us."[18] She maintains that, in order to counter the mass movements and emotions that threaten the survival of the species, the human race must learn to understand group behavior, to take a long view of its own evolution, to grasp the continuing threat of reversion to the barbarism of group behavior endemic to the species since the human race first became differentiated from animals; an image of this behavior occurs in the character of Ben, the throwback in *The Fifth Child,* who epitomizes the reversion to brutality and group primacy. She suggests that writers (she primarily means fiction writers), because of their habits of observation and examination, are more likely to be able to detach themselves from group feeling. Further, writers everywhere "together making up a whole . . . are . . . aspects of a function that has been evolved by society"[19] in the interests of species survival.

## Notes

1. Lessing, introduction, *The Golden Notebook* (New York: Simon and Schuster, 1962) xi.

2. Marion Vlastos, "Doris Lessing and R. D. Laing: Psychopolitics and Prophecy," *Critical Essays on Doris Lessing*, ed. Claire Sprague and Virginia Tiger (Boston: Hall, 1986) 127.

3. Katherine Fishburn, "Wor(l)ds Within Words: Doris Lessing as Meta-Fictionist and Metaphysician," *Studies in the Novel* 20 (Summer 1988): 187.

4. Nissa Torrents, "Doris Lessing: Testament to Mysticism," trans. Paul Schlueter, *Doris Lessing Newsletter* 4.2 (Winter 1980): 12.

5. Eve Bertelsen, "Who Is It Who Says 'I'?: The Persona of a Doris Lessing Interview," *Doris Lessing: The Alchemy of Survival*, ed. Carey Kaplan and Ellen Cronan Rose, (Athens: Ohio University Press, 1988) 179.

6. Betsy Draine, *Substance under Pressure: Artistic Coherence and Evolving Forms in the Novels of Doris Lessing* (Madison: University of Wisconsin Press, 1983) xi.

7. Draine xiv.

8. Lessing, *Landlocked;* (New York: Simon and Schuster, 1966) 302.

9. Frederick Karl, "The Four-Gaited Beast of the Apocalypse: Doris Lessing's *The Four-Gated City*," *Old Lines, New Forces: Essays on the Contemporary British Novel*, ed. Robert K. Morris (Rutherford, NJ: Fairleigh Dickinson, 1976) 183.

10. For further discussion of Lessing's image of the city, see Jean Pickering, "Marxism and Madness: The Two Faces of Doris Lessing's Myth," *Modern Fiction Studies* 26 (Spring 1980): 17–30; Ellen Cronan Rose, "Doris Lessing's *Città Felice*," *Critical Essays on Doris Lessing* 141–53; and Mary Ann Singleton, *The City and the Veld: The Fiction of Doris Lessing* (Lewisburg, PA: Bucknell University Press, 1977).

11. Lessing, *The Four-Gated City* (New York: Knopf, 1969) 288.

12. For an excellent analysis of the relations between the individ-

## OVERVIEW

ual, the collective, and the whole, see Mona Knapp, *Doris Lessing* (New York: Ungar, 1984) 9–10.

13. Claire Sprague, *Rereading Doris Lessing* (Chapel Hill: University of North Carolina Press, 1987) 5–6.

14. Lessing, *The Memoirs of a Survivor* (New York: Knopf, 1975).

15. Roy Newquist, "Interview with Doris Lessing," *A Small Personal Voice,* ed. Paul Schlueter (New York: Knopf, 1974) 49.

16. Dee Seligman, "The Four-Faced Novelist," *Modern Fiction Studies* 26 (Spring 1980): 16.

17. Lessing, "The Small Personal Voice," *A Small Personal Voice,* 20–1.

18. Lessing, *Prisons We Choose to Live Inside* (New York: Harper, 1987) 7.

19. Lessing, *Prisons* 8.

# CHAPTER TWO

# *The Grass Is Singing* (1950); *African Stories* (1964)

*The Grass Is Singing* was written before Lessing left Rhodesia and published the year after she emigrated to England, where she wrote most of the stories later collected as *African Stories*. The interrelatedness of her work, so evident later in her career, was apparent even at this early period. The relations between the individual and the collective (by which Lessing means both institutions, like marriage or the educational system, and groups one elects to join, like a sports club or the Communist Party), between black and white, between men and women, between the settler and the land, between role and identity, and between the Freudian "nightmare repetition"[1] and the Jungian task of individuation are related themes appearing in both the novel and the stories.[2]

In the preface to *African Stories* Lessing says, "When my first novel, *The Grass Is Singing*, came out, there were few novels about Africa. That book, and my second, *This Was the Old Chief's Country*, were described by reviewers as about the colour problem . . . which is not how I see, or saw, them."[3] Now at some remove from the newness of such overt discussion of race relations, it is easier to appreciate the complexity Lessing intended in *The Grass Is Singing*, which like her later works is a novel resistant to a single interpretation.

At the most obvious level it depicts a complex clash of value systems. Although the white settlers grew up in a class society, which may as in the case of Charlie Slatter still affect their personal relationships, the class attitudes of the collective have simplified into considerations of us, the whites, and them, the blacks. Other class gradations, such as exist in England, fade before this one great chasm. But there is another value system that complicates the issue. In white settler society men outrank women even more than they do at "Home" in middle-class England. Charlie Slatter can make a joke of this situation: "Niggers . . . keep their own women in the right place."[4] This "natural" relationship of dominant man and submissive woman becomes problematic in this society only when the man is black and the woman white: clearly if the sexes are reversed, there is no difficulty at all. Several of the characters in *African Stories* have bush wives—Captain Stocker of "The Black Madonna" and Leopard George from the story of that name, for example—without reproach from the collective. In 1978 Michael Thorpe noted that "since 1903 in Rhodesia it has been a criminal offence for a black man and white woman to have sexual intercourse but no such law applies where a white man and a black woman are involved."[5] This law recognizes that the relationship between white woman and black man is a point of tension, a weakness in colonial culture; and because black men rather than black women take jobs as domestic servants, the weak spot in the social system lies within the white man's home. Thus women especially must abide by the "esprit de corps," a rule that Mary Turner inadvertently violates.

Charlie Slatter, spokesman for the collective, demonstrates how colonialism brutalizes, how easy it is for the oppressed to become the oppressor—a process that by the end of the novel has also overtaken Moses, the Turners' houseboy. Slatter, from the British underclass, a "proper cockney," an ex-grocer's assistant, dominates his wife and his sons (whom he raises as "gentlemen," a class of persons he both despises and admires). The complexities of his character are developed at greater length in "Getting Off the Altitude," where his drive to domination takes sexual expression. His special fear, shared by the entire British community, is that one of them will go under, slide into hopeless poverty, for example, or otherwise demonstrate to the blacks the essential similarity of the races. In *The Grass Is Singing* only Mary Turner comes close to perceiving this common humanity, and then only in the twisted forms of mental breakdown. Macintosh, the mine owner of "The Antheap," is forced to face it directly when Tommy Clarke, the white boy who seems like a son to him, refuses to attend the university unless Macintosh's illegitimate coloured[6] son can go as well.

The beginning of *The Grass Is Singing* invokes the genre of the traditional murder mystery, although it establishes the identity of the murderer in the newspaper item that announces the murder, included as an epigraph to the first chapter. The item also establishes the stereotypic collective response, which is elaborated in the first chapter by an omniscient narrator. The overwhelming question, which the old colonials who have "become used to the country" (22) are determined to ignore, focuses on motivation. The collective here comprises the long-time British settlers, who have rigid codes on which they depend to keep their errant compatriots as well as the natives in line. The negative effect of such a collective on the individual is seen in "The Black Madonna," where Captain Stocker, who must hide his tears from the nurse, is jeered into silence by his wife, "My little Hitler, . . . my Storm-trooper." (AS18). This story suggests a positive alternative to the collective in the figure of an Italian painter, whose experiences as soldier and prisoner of war have put him in touch with his feelings. There is no such positive alternative to the rigidity of the collective in *The Grass Is Singing*, where, when the Turners reject the collective, they both in their different ways slip into alienation and madness.

In the first chapter of the novel Lessing uses Tony

Marston, fresh out from England, to pose the questions the collective deliberately ignores. But he focuses on the personal histories of the Turners as though the collective is not implicated in their tragedy. He believes that to understand the murder, "the important thing . . . [is] to understand the background, the circumstances, the characters of Dick and Mary, the pattern of their lives" (17). The second chapter, switching away from the collective view of chapter 1, begins a chronological account of Mary's life by an omniscient narrator, although, as the narrative progresses, events are increasingly presented from Mary's point of view. This account continues for the next eight chapters, bringing the narrative up to the evening of the day before the murder, at which point there is a return to the collective view of the situation in the Turner household. The novel completes the circle, finally describing the events immediately before the first chapter. This last chapter stays close to Mary's point of view until the machete blow that brings her down, a structure that underscores the sense of inevitable repetition increasingly articulated throughout the novel. The narrative changes to omniscient narration in the last two paragraphs, which are focused on Moses.

The opinion of the collective is that Moses murdered Mary Turner for stereotypical reasons, in the course of a robbery, for example. They interpret it in the context of the master-servant relationship—in short, as a race matter. Early readings of the novel, which emphasized the race question, led to the conclusion that Mary represents the entire white race, or at least the British segment of it. But Lessing has guarded against this simplistic view by making the murder victim a woman. In light of the complexity of Lessing's later works, it seems clear that neither the problem of race nor that of gender can be subordinated to the other: Lessing has not made Mary a woman in order to suggest that, in Moses's dominating her, he represents the superior masculinity of the blacks, even though Tony Marston does believe that one of the foundations of "the colour bar . . . is the jealousy of the white man for the superior sexual potency of the native" (220). Nor has she made Moses a man in order to suggest that the novel's main focus is female oppression. Rather, it seems that women and blacks are both oppressed by the collective, the dominant white male British culture. Yet, as the adolescent girl of "The Old Chief Mshangla" realizes, to say that "I could not help it. I am also a victim" (AS56) simply won't do. Further, blaming individual British settlers is too simplistic to explain the case of Dick Turner, a victim if ever there was one, a victim of his bullying father, of his own visionary nature, of his own dreams, his own poor grasp of cause and effect.

Throughout Lessing's African writings the farm that means freedom for a white man—freedom from the life of a clerk, of an employee, freedom from the restrictions of suburban England or from the poverty of the working class—means prison for his wife, even when the farm is successful, as in "The De Wets Come to Kloof Grange" or "Getting Off the Altitude." Dick's love of the farm means imprisonment for Mary; she realizes that she will never leave, no matter how prosperous the farm becomes. Ironically, Mary's only chance to leave comes too late, when social pressure forces Dick—now poised on the edge of bankruptcy—to sell the farm to Charlie Slatter so that he can take his disturbed wife for an extended holiday. Like Alec, the visionary of "Eldorado," who begins to believe he can divine gold much as a water diviner detects water, and his wife Maggie, who clings to the idea of education as a way of "getting on," Dick and Mary Turner each have their conflicting inner worlds, but neither is strong enough either to support or to subsume the other's vision. As Kenneth of "Winter in July" says, "In a marriage it's necessary for one side to be strong enough to create the illusion" (AS246)—which Maggie, out of a kind of maternal pity, manages to do for Alec. "The Second Hut" posits a situation very similar to that of Dick and Mary Turner. Major Carruthers escaped from the domination of his successful brother in England to a farm in Africa, where every year he and his wife, a middle-class Englishwoman, slide deeper into poverty. Although he is by no means impervious to his wife's sufferings and the hardships he imposes on his two boys, he resists the knowledge that her illness—physical rather than mental as in Mary Turner's case—would clear up if he left the farm. Both the Carruthers understand their situation;

neither is driven by unconscious motivation, and the major foresees the consequences of his choice. Even so, it takes the appalling example of his Boer assistant's careless attitude toward the abject poverty in which he supports a wife and numerous children to make the major write to his brother for help. For Mrs. Carruthers release is the return to England, whereas for Mary Turner it is life in the city of her young womanhood; in both cases freedom is a return to the life before marriage.

The narrator's account of Mary's childhood gives the facts of her psychological development, but their full impact becomes clear only as her situation, increasingly approximating her mother's, reawakens her repressed emotions, which appear in dreams occurring more frequently as she sinks into madness. The seeds of her breakdown were sown years before Dick brings her to the farm. When her breakdown is far advanced, it becomes clear that its roots lie in her childhood experience. As a young woman she represses the memories of traumatic experiences and makes a safe life for herself. She is happy as an efficient secretary, as a valued elder member of the club for unmarried girls where she lives; she has many men friends, with whom she assiduously avoids sexual entanglements. This life is destroyed by the collective insistence on marriage for women. The fragile self she has built disintegrates when she overhears some of her friends criticizing her too-young clothes, laughing because sexuality seems left out of her makeup: "She just isn't like that, isn't like that at all. Something missing somewhere" (39). Because Mary knows so little about herself, what she overhears destroys her self-image, which she is unable to re-create. Instead, the vast hollowness that will later overwhelm her makes its first appearance: "she was hollow inside, empty, and into this emptiness would sweep from nowhere a vast panic, as if there were nothing in the world she could grasp hold of" (43). In this hollow state she becomes oversensitive to what others are thinking and marries Dick out of a desperate need for a husband to release her from the life she has built—a life she later looks back on as ideal.

At first, though frigid with Dick, she is happy enough on the farm, enjoying "putting things to rights and making a little go a long way" (64–65). She desperately tries to make an environment for herself, fixing up the wretched two-room house as comfortably as her small savings allow. Her energy and efficiency alarm Dick, first because he himself lacks these qualities and second because he does not see how she will keep herself occupied. This same efficiency so useful for whitewashing walls and running up curtains out of flour sacks makes her relations with successive houseboys hostile. When the heat, beating through the corrugated iron roof, undermines her, she begins to complain in a new voice "taken direct from her mother," a voice that is not her own but that of "the suffering female" (86). According to Freudian theory, only self-knowledge can prevent the neurotic repetition of an unhealthy family pattern—which knowledge is clearly beyond Mary's capacities. When Dick insists that Mary work in the kaffir store he builds, she recognizes in his plan the repetition of her childhood nightmare; to argue with it would have been like "arguing with destiny itself" (105). The only way she can break the cycle is to run away to the city. As her old boss refuses to give her a job, she returns to the farm with Dick, which binds him "to her in gratitude forever" (117). The emptiness again invading her, she touches the earth to reassure herself that she exists and takes pleasure in shivering when the rains come, an extreme awareness of her environment that returns to her in her last crisis. She tries to face her future with "a tired stoicism" (115) related to her sense of inevitability.

Another disruption comes into their relationship when Dick contracts malaria. Supervising the laborers in his absence, Mary hits a "magnificently built" native across the face with a sjambok. Although she regards the native as "cheeky," she is as surprised by the blow as he is. His marvelous body, Lessing suggests, both frightens Mary and challenges her to try to dominate him. The fear of his physical power and of her own sexual impulses, combined with her frustration at Dick's inability to run the farm, challenge her to dominate the native.

But her response to the man is not merely personal. Her views on the proper relation of the races are those of the collective extreme: "her greatest anger was directed against the sentimentalists and theoreticians . . . who interfered with the natural right of a white farmer to treat his labour as he pleased" (136). Dick himself, a far more humane boss than Mary, speaks in much the same terms, though neither is as violent as Charlie Slatter, who was fined thirty pounds for killing one of his laborers in a fit of anger.

The "arid feminism" (33) Mary inherited from her mother has given her a feeling of superiority over men, which she has been unable to sustain since she became dependent on Dick. Only in relationship to black male servants and laborers can she press her will to victory over men in general because, after all, the collective condones it. Her desire to dominate Dick is ambivalent because of collective values; she believes she would respect a man who stood up to her, as the mores of the collective demand. No matter how feeble her husband, no matter how incompetent in comparison with herself, the relationship between them must appear to be based on male dominance: "When she saw him weak and goalless, and pitiful, she hated him, and the hate turned in on herself. She needed a man stronger than herself, and she was trying to create one out of Dick" (145). When the tobacco she bullies him into planting succumbs to drought, she finally collapses into despair, knowing that her life will never change.

For a short time she understands everything about her situation without illusion, "seeing herself and Dick and their relationship to each other and to the farm, and their future, without a shadow of false hope, as honest and stark as the truth itself." In this mood she recognizes that Dick is a nice man who "did not try to get his own back" (157) when she makes him suffer. She cannot maintain this painful clarity of vision for long and gives way to an inertia so great that if she is thirsty she cannot fetch a glass of water or call the servant to bring one.

This inertia moves rapidly into breakdown under the influence of the Turners' next houseboy. When Dick brings in a field hand to be trained, Mary recognizes the scar across his face. Although she pleads for another boy, Dick insists on Moses, whom she reluctantly accepts. In spite of her efforts to maintain a master-servant relationship, a personal relationship develops, at least in part because she cannot forget the moment of fear after she hit him. This fear is not simply of his "powerful, broad-built body," not even fear of black men in general, but of unknown Africa itself and, echoing Conrad, the impulses in herself the dark continent represents. In Jungian terms Moses comes to represent her shadow, that part of the unconscious where repressed elements of the personality accumulate.

As her madness progresses, she explicitly equates Moses with the bush. This relationship between the bush and the native is most completely worked out in "The Old Chief Mshlanga," where the young narrator articulates her fear, calling it the "shapeless menace"

(AS53). She recognizes that what she feels is the terror of isolation, which is clearly Mary's condition. In this context, it is clear why Moses comes to represent all the fears of Mary's life. When she accidentally catches sight of him naked from waist up, she again feels fear and is "jerked clean out of her apathy" (166).

Becoming an automaton, she obsesses on Moses: "the knowledge of that man alone in the house with her lay like a weight at the back of her mind," which dwindles into "a soft aching blank" (171–72). The only part of it still awake is the one responsive to him. When he wants to leave the farm, she bursts into tears and begs him to stay. Now Moses starts to become a father figure: his voice as he pushes her down onto the bed is "gentle, . . . almost fatherly." She dwells on this voice, "firm and kind, like a father commanding her" (175–76). Mary tries to resume her angry tone to Moses, but he does not allow her to depersonalize him in this fashion, insisting that she treat him like a human being. When she refuses to eat, he brings her, unbidden, eggs, tea, jam, with a cup of bush flowers on the tray. His evident desire to please disturbs her, making her feel helplessly in his power; the omniscient narrator explains that she suffers from an unacknowledged, unrecognized "dark attraction" (179). She dreams of him standing over her, "powerful and commanding, yet kind, but forcing her into a position where she had to touch him" (181). She dreams of her own father in a nightmare with the quality of a repressed memory: he holds her face down in his lap with "his small hairy hands," and his "un-washed masculine smell" makes her feel she is suffocat-ing (190). Moses becomes identified not only with the father function but with her actual father: she joyfully dreams that Dick is dead, that Moses, comforting her protectively, is also "her father menacing and horrible, [touching] her in desire" (192). A sense of fate, of inevi-tability, connected with the nightmare of repetition that imprisons Mary on the farm in spite of her happy, inde-pendent young womanhood in the city overwhelms her: "she felt as if she were in a dark tunnel, nearing something final, something she could not visualize, but which waited for her inexorably, inescapably" (195).

Having brought the reader increasingly closer to Mary's state of mind, both conscious and unconscious, the narrative now reverts to the outside view of the first chapter, and the collective perception resumes. Al-though Mary never acknowledges a sexual relationship with Moses, the outsiders through whose eyes the ac-tion of the penultimate chapter is presented interpret Mary's behavior as sexual. Charlie Slatter is distressed by her disturbed coquetry when, dressed again in girl-ish clothes, she flirts with him; he is even more dis-tressed when he hears her talk to Moses in the same tone. Marston, the outsider new from England, is amazed when he realizes that Moses dresses and un-dresses her with an air of "indulgent uxoriousness" (219). She accuses Marston: "It was all right till you came!" (223). Marston sees that nothing he can say will bring her back into the collective frame of mind: "She has forgotten what her own people are like" (221). He cannot know that she has always had trouble with the collective, whose insistence on marriage, combined with her ignorance of her own nature, is largely responsible for her circumstances.

In the last two chapters Mary's reactions, whether seen from without, as in the penultimate, or from within, as in the last, show clear dissociation. Her madness grows both from her years-long repression and from the irreconcilability of her desires. She has internalized the color bar, which makes her desire for Moses inadmissible even to herself; further, she associates him with her father. The two sexual relationships most vehemently forbidden by the collective thus in Mary's mind intersect in Moses.

Her disintegration, the first of many analyses of madness by Lessing, is the most powerful piece of writing in the novel. Her apathy dissipated, Mary runs through a great variety of emotions, becoming aware of the feelings she has repressed. She wakes "vastly peaceful and rested" (224) on what she knows will be her last day. Her complicity in her own death is clear, suggesting a suicidal tendency of which she herself seems unaware. Certainly death seems to be the only possible resolution of her conflicting impulses. She attains a larger vision than she has ever approached before, seeing the farm, "that immensely pitiable thing" (225), from a great distance; her vision extends to the

### THE GRASS IS SINGING; AFRICAN STORIES

future, in which she sees the house steadily killed by the bush, "which had always hated it" (231). From peace she runs through irritation, joy, panic, hope of rescue, pride, terror, and acceptance. Just as she considered the nightmare of repetition unavoidable in spite of her conscious intentions, so she believes her death inevitable, the logical outcome of her situation.

Like Mary's, Moses's motives are complex, and seem the more so because his mental processes are never directly shown. On the one hand he seems genuinely concerned about Mary when he first insists on a human relationship; on the other, he appears to revel in his mastery over her, even in front of Charlie Slatter, who notices his "conscious power" (208–9). He looks at Tony Marston, the apparent cause of his dismissal and Mary's planned departure, with a most unsubmissive "malevolent glare" (219). The last paragraph suggests revenge on Marston as a possible motive for killing Mary, because Dick "had been defeated long ago" (244). The narrator, however, specifically refuses to name Moses's frame of mind, which may include "thoughts of regret, or pity, or perhaps even wounded human affection" (245). His reactions to Mary have been varied: anger when she strikes him, resentment when she is cross toward him, tender when she is sick, bullying when she, shamed because of the judgments against her by Slatter and Marston, tries to send him away. In speculating upon what Michael Thorpe calls "the incomprehensible workings of the 'native' mind,"[7]

## UNDERSTANDING DORIS LESSING

Lessing deliberately avoids tying down the motivation too glibly: she has no aversion to describing the thought processes of Africans, as "Hunger" demonstrates. Jabavu, the story's central character, has a psychological history as complex as that of Moses, with an equally powerful love-hate relationship to the white man's way of life. She reveals the hungers feeding Jabavu's dreams, however, while Moses's remain hidden. In thus avoiding a total emphasis on cause and effect, a dictum that the murder of Mary is a direct result of social circumstances and deterministic psychology even while she suggests its inevitability, Lessing refuses to blame the collective in order to exonerate the individual. Influenced by the existentialism of the post-World War Two years, she maintains that individuals cannot take refuge in collective judgment but must take responsibility for the conditions of their existence. As Orphia Jane Allen says, for Lessing "the prerequisite . . . for freedom is the *choice* of a creative mean between alienation and the mindlessness of the collective."[8] Because she does not understand that "she was made to live, by nature and upbringing, alone and sufficient to herself" (115), Mary, missing the "creative mean" altogether, manages to fall victim to both extremes.

Yet the final chapter indicates that Mary has some insight into the cause of her breakdown. From the beginning, readers have known that spiritual sterility is the main theme of the novel. The epigraph from T. S. Eliot's "The Waste Land," from which the title is taken, highlights the symbolic relevance of Mary's hatred of the enervating heat, the seasonal dryness that can be alleviated only by the rains. In the last chapter Mary's thoughts become imbued with the language of traditional Christianity: words like *vigil, prophecy, evil, innocence, salvation, guilt,* and *sin* appear. This vocabulary should not surprise in view of Mary's and Moses's names. Mary is named after both the virgin and the whore, the mother of Jesus and Mary Magdalene. Moses in murdering Mary suggests a future in which the blacks will oust the whites and regain a land of their own; like the biblical Moses he points toward a promised land that he himself will never enter. Mary's death thus carries both public and private implications of regeneration. Her vision of the bush taking over the house suggests the possibility, fully explored in *Briefing for a Descent into Hell* and *The Golden Notebook,* of mental breakdown as a healing mechanism. For Mary her realization is too late, but her perception that the rains will come after her death indicates that she finally understands her sterility of spirit.

This sterility of spirit, however, is not the cause of her breakdown, which is prompted by resistance to self-knowledge. A quick comparison with "Winter in July," which is also about the evil of spiritual sterility, will clarify the point. Like Mary, Julia has a vision of evil, but at a much earlier stage in her life. It is the word she uses to name rootlessness, impermanence, a life without meaning. Rejecting the vision as "the result of being tired, and nearly thirty," (AS221), she marries the elder of two half-brothers, eventually becoming "a kind of high-class concubine to the two of [them]" (AS245). Like Mary's, her situation has its roots in a childhood trauma, but in Julia's case the trauma is her husband's: "I suppose you must have been very jealous of [Kenneth], that was it, wasn't it?" (AS233). Tom's real interest is not, like Dick's, the farm, but his half-brother Kenneth; he connives at the relationship between his wife and his brother because he wants to keep Kenneth on the farm. In short, he sells out his wife in much the same way that Dick sells out Mary; both men see their wives as accessories to some other need. Julia resents, much as Mary might if she had the intellectual capacity to phrase it thus, "the way they took their women into their lives, without changing a thought or a habit to meet them" (AS243). Mary blames Dick's ineptitude and consequent poverty for the failure of their marriage—after all, money was the only thing her parents quarreled about, though they did so frequently. The brothers' farm is prosperous to the point of wealth, but the evil recurring at the end of "Winter in July" is the same sterility that Mary recognizes in the last chapter of *The Grass Is Singing*. Julia is just as emotionally isolated, just as alienated, as Mary. Both women in the moment of crisis have a heightened sensitivity to the African landscape, to which they recognize they are strangers. What saves Julia from breakdown, though not from alienation, is her capacity for self-knowledge.

## THE GRASS IS SINGING; AFRICAN STORIES

Mary has based her identity on roles assigned by various collectives rather than on her own nature; when the gap between outer and inner becomes too great, she disintegrates into the madness that invites her death.

## Notes

1. Lessing, *A Proper Marriage* (New York: Simon and Schuster, 1962) 337.

2. For a full discussion of individuation see C. G. Jung, *Man and His Symbols* (New York: Doubleday, 1964).

3. Lessing, *African Stories* (New York: Simon and Schuster, 1965)

5. Subsequent references to this volume will be noted AS in parentheses.

4. Lessing, *The Grass Is Singing* (New York: Crowell, 1950) 19. Subsequent references will be noted in parentheses.

5. Michael Thorpe, *Doris Lessing's Africa* (London: Evans Brothers, 1978) 12 n.

6. *Coloured* is the southern African word for an individual of mixed racial parentage or an Indian.

7. Thorpe 14.

8. Orphia Jane Allen, "Structure and Motif in Doris Lessing's *A Man and Two Women,*" *Modern Fiction Studies* 26 (Spring 1980): 74.

# CHAPTER THREE

# *Children of Violence*

The implications of the themes of *The Grass Is Singing* are further explored in *Children of Violence*, a five-volume narrative centered on the developing consciousness of Martha Quest from her adolescence in Zambesia (a fictional composite of several southern African countries) to her middle years in London and her death on a small island off the coast of Scotland. In reference to this sequence Lessing first articulated her interest in the tension between the individual and society, pointing out that it is "a study of the individual conscience in its relations with the collective."[1] Although Martha Quest is subject to the same social pressures, because of her superior capacity for intellectual and spiritual growth she resists the repetition that trapped Mary Turner.

Lessing points out in an afterword that *The Four-Gated City* constitutes a *Bildungsroman*,[2] a kind of novel documenting the growth—the building—of the protagonist's character through a succession of social interactions; critics have generally assumed that her observation refers to the sequence as a whole. The narrative, as Martha's family name suggests, is structured by her search to find herself. This search focuses on the answers to two fundamental questions that occupy Martha throughout her life: What constitutes the individual—that is, what is identity? What is its proper relation to the collective and the whole? The sequence provides an inclusive dialogue answering these questions, which appear in several related guises.

Martha's given name suggests the complementary side of her nature, the practical as opposed to the philosophic. Like her biblical namesake Martha is characterized by service, by the kind of attention necessary to keep an organization or a home running. Lessing provides a gloss on the name: "an image of willing, adaptable, intelligent service."[3] This side of Martha's character does not become obvious till the later volumes, first manifesting itself in her service to the Marxist group in the middle volumes of the series, beginning with the concluding section of *A Proper Marriage*, and appearing full-blown in the domestic and nurturant form traditionally deemed feminine in *The Four-Gated City*.

This discrepancy between her given and family names is further complicated by a gap between the two forms of her given name. *Matty*, which friends and relations call her in the early volumes, is the name Martha assigns to the clumsy, apologetic, clowning self who appears in response to the demands of unwelcome social roles, while she reserves *Martha* for the detached, constant observer who watches and evaluates both herself and her environment.

This gap between the outer and inner Martha is reflected in the narrative style. The distance between protagonist and narrator makes Martha's youthful naïveté subject to ironic comment. The appeal is to recognition of rather than identification with the young Martha's follies, which belong to a stage of life most readers have outgrown, their response thus being an amused sympathy.

### *Martha Quest* (1952; covering the years 1934–38)

In *Martha Quest* appear two images of integration, unity, and wholeness that recur through the sequence, both of which come from Martha's psychological core. The first—so important it haunts her all her life—gives the title to the last novel of the series, *The Four-Gated City*. She summons "the familiar day dream" as a talisman against the fragmentation of the human condition. Built in the veld she imagines

a noble city, set foursquare and colonnaded along its falling, flower-bordered terraces. There were splashing fountains and the sounds of flutes; and its citizens moved, grave and beautiful, black and white and brown

## CHILDREN OF VIOLENCE

together; and these groups of elders paused, and smiled with pleasure at the sight of the children—the blue-eyed, fair-skinned children of the North playing hand in hand with the bronze-skinned, dark-eyed children of the South.[4]

This image reappears throughout the sequence not only in Martha's mind but also in the language of other characters, and in many forms, in parodic or inverted variations, but recognizably this "fabulous and ancient city." It is an image of individual wholeness as well as social unity; further, it suggests Martha's desire for an egalitarian society as well as for a nurturant authority, something lacking in her own experience both in her parents and in the Establishment, represented for her by the threatening figure of Judge Maynard.

The second recurring image is of the veld, a place where Martha has the first stirrings of visionary experience. Here she feels at one with her environment rather than at odds with it, which is her usual condition:

There was a slow integration, during which she, and the little animals, and the moving grasses, and the sun-warmed trees, and the slopes of shivering silver meal-ies, and the great dome of blue light overhead, and the stones of earth under her feet, became one, shuddering together in a dissolution of dancing atoms. She felt the rivers under the ground forcing themselves painfully along her veins, swelling them in an unbearable pressure; her flesh was the earth, and suffered growth like a ferment, and her eyes stared, fixed like the eye of the sun. (62)

The veld represents the primary unity to which humanity belonged before evolving into self-conscious beings, where the individual may feel integrated with the universe. Landscapes, even single trees, may invoke this feeling in Martha years later when she lives in London, the very antithesis of the veld.

The oneness with nature Martha sometimes experiences on the veld occurs also in such stories as "Sunrise on the Veld" and, in a negative way, in Mary Turner's final image of the bush taking over the Turner farm. Thus Mary's madness is a perverse version of Martha's heightened consciousness, a consciousness Martha herself associates with what she calls her "religious phase" (61), just as real cities such as Salisbury and London are perverse versions of Martha's ideal city.

However, unity in itself is not enough. As Mary Ann Singleton points out, the price of nature's unity is the renunciation of a distinctively human feature, self-consciousness. Only by negating consciousness can one return to the instinctive life that entails submitting to "the ceaseless round of natural repetition, all instinct with no reason."[5] Thus Martha visualizes a city built in the veld so that it may be influenced by but rise above this primeval unity that sacrifices the individual to the collective good: "The City in the veld is a man-made harmony—part of nature, yet at the same time separate from it, as consciousness is of and yet above nature."[6]

While the city in the veld is an image of the integration of the individual with the whole, it is also an image of the integration of the personality. Throughout the sequence the inner state and the outer state reflect each other, the intimate relationship between them becoming more overt as the sequence progresses. In *Martha Quest*, Martha has hostile reactions to almost everyone she meets, reflecting her acute state of self-division. But the issue is larger than a classic case of adolescent projection: Zambesian society is also deeply divided with the British, Afrikaners, Jews, Greeks, native Africans all living in a state of permanent alienation. In fact, the social division seems as much a cause as a corollary of Martha's self-division.

On the threshold of adult collective life, Martha tries to define herself by rejecting various prescribed roles, particularly her mother's plans and her mother's example. She resists Mrs. Quest's desire to make her into a nice young English girl, pre-First World War model. Disturbed by her daughter's budding sexuality, Mrs. Quest wants to keep Martha a child. With unerring instinct Martha flaunts her copy of "Havelock Ellis on sex," the best-known sex manual of the 30s. She resents the expectation that she will "play the part of 'young girl'" (12) complementing the role of the matron—the kind of person she resents and fears until she becomes middle-aged herself.

Because the life she sees around her offers her so few roles for women, she falls back on literature, searching for some defining comment on her situation. She finds it not in the nineteenth-century novels she prefers but in the more sober works she borrows from the intellectual Cohen brothers. From them she gains "a clear picture of herself," which also suggests the scope of *Children of Violence:*

She was adolescent, and therefore bound to be unhappy; British, and therefore uneasy and defensive; in the fourth decade of the twentieth century, and therefore inescapably beset with problems of race and class; female, and obliged to repudiate the shackled women of the past. (18)

The Cohens' books also tell her that her life is determined by heredity, by the trauma of being born, or by the first five years of life; in any case they all convey the message "of fate, of doom" (19). She interprets this inevitability as entrapment. As the foregoing quotation indicates, entrapment comes from various forces most conveniently summarized by *biology, history,* and *society.* The "swollen bodies" of pregnant women arouse in her a "shuddering anger, as at the sight of a cage designed for herself" (67). Much of the resentment directed at her mother comes from her suspicion that she may grow to be like Mrs. Quest. Perceiving the life cycle as the most extreme instance of necessity, she sees entrapment specifically as repetition of the past, of the patterns formed by biology and history, which manifest themselves to her most oppressively as the expectations of society. On this point she is in real, permanent disagreement with her parents and most of their generation, who look to the past for behavioral models, because her lifelong commitment, no matter what form it takes, is to the future.

Although Martha rejects some prescribed roles, she tries to conform to others. Considering her indignant feminism, it is ironic that her sense of self is bound up with the image of a man. She tries out her idea of herself against a whole series: Billy, the brother of a childhood friend; Donovan, a latent homosexual who tries to make Martha into a fashion plate; Dolly (short for the ominous Adolph), with whom Martha has her first sexual experience, not because of passion but because her repulsion at anti-Semitism leads her into a false situation. When the fever of war sweeps through the colony, setting off an explosion of marriage and parenthood for an entire generation, she marries at nineteen the civil servant Douglas Knowell, even though she goes to the ceremony in a state of profound disbelief, exhibiting "passive compliance accompanied by repressed hostility."[7] Although she longs for consistency, for rational control, she suffers from a fluidity of personality: "it was as if half a dozen entirely different people inhabited her body, and they violently disliked each other, bound together by only one thing, a strong pulse of longing;

anonymous, impersonal, formless, like water" (153). These divisions alarm her because she perceives that feelings not under her control will trap her in situations she wants to avoid, of which her marriage to Douglas is a prime example.

One incident suggests that nonetheless she believes there is a stable component to her so-far undifferentiated personality. She covets a dark blue evening dress whose full skirts are scattered with rhinestones: in it "she would be revealed to herself, and to others, as something quite new, but deeply herself" (151). Although on this occasion she does not buy the dress, it is clearly the one she wears for Thomas Stern, the one man with whom she has a real relationship, described in *Landlocked.* This episode typifies Martha's idea of her identity at this stage in her life: that it already exists if only she could find it—that it might be called into being but not created by circumstances, by a man, a dress, a group of people. It indicates, albeit ironically, Martha's sense that her self exists apart from her social function, which later develops into her determination to work for spiritual growth, on what Jung calls the task of individuation.

Nonetheless Martha persists in thinking that joining the right collective, in which "people altogether generous and warm exchanged generous emotions" (130), will help her actualize herself. At the Sports Club the young people do everything collectively; their behavior is rigidly prescribed even though the rules are not formally articulated. As the function of the club is in fact to preserve itself as a group, all activities must be public: "anything was permissible, the romances, the flirtations, the quarrels, provided they were shared" (147). Consummated sexual relationships are eschewed in favor of what was called "heavy petting" in the United States in the 50s—an activity that disgusts Martha, who feels it her right to lose her virginity as quickly as possible. Although she does not endorse the Sports Club norms, nonetheless she succumbs to them, getting carried along by the group.

This group, because of the age of its members, is especially vulnerable to the tides of twentieth-century history, which is subject to the same kind of inevitability as the biological cycle: at the Sports Club, during the celebrations of the "last Christmas" (179) before World War Two, everyone senses, "like a frightening wind, a feeling of necessity" (180). And this necessity is not altogether disagreeable; even Martha falls victim to it, imagining herself a nurse (as her mother was), "a heroine in the trenches" overseas (178).

Martha's parents, especially Mrs. Quest, labor under their own version of necessity. They are convinced that Martha is getting married because she is pregnant, which suggestion outrages Martha—the more so since Mrs. Quest triumphantly assumes that now Martha will have to settle into a conventional life. But Martha has no such expectation: she resumes "that other journey of discovery which alternated with the discoveries of a young woman loose in town; she returned to her books" (209–10), evaluating everything she reads by the question: "What has this got to do with me?" She has an overwhelming touchstone to judge by: "that experience . . . which was the gift of her solitary childhood on the veld" (210). At the end of *Martha Quest* she is still searching for the answers to her questions about the nature of the individual and the collective, which she has not found in sex, in her work at the law firm, or in either the Left Book Club or the Sports Club. Nor does she feel hopeful that she will find them as the wife of Douglas Knowell; in fact, a few days before the wedding she overhears a voice "remarking calmly within her that she would not stay married to him" (253).

### *A Proper Marriage* (1954; covering the years 1939–41)

The interactions of biological and historical necessity dominate the action of *A Proper Marriage*. Both these forces bring the loss of individuality, the first through the impersonality of nature as exemplified by the veld, the second through an overriding collective of patriotic feeling. This novel demonstrates how collectives can be built on biology so that, in the case of women especially, social constraints are made to seem natural.

These forces pressure Martha into various collectives, the first of which is marriage, the second motherhood. Love, that image promoted both by books and society, has in collusion with the sex drive brought Martha, at the age of nineteen, to "lie beside"[8] Douglas Knowell regardless of her determination not to marry; as the opening chapter makes clear, she is already pregnant in spite of her resolution never to become a mother. A ferris wheel visible from their bedroom window, "a chain of lights that mingled with the lamps of Orion and the Cross" (284), reminding her of a wedding ring, comes to symbolize the cycle of repetition. Yet while she perceives Douglas as an agent of entrapment, she still retains the pattern of seeing a man as an avenue to freedom: "What she actually wanted, of course, was for some man to arrive in her life, simply take her by the hand, and lead her off into [a] new world" (329)—a pattern of expectation she retains until she finally leaves the colony for England in *The Four-Gated City*.

The variety of her emotions gives her "a sense of being used by something impersonal and irresistible" (318), a sensation later echoed in her affair with Thomas Stern, the only man who ever touches her psychological core to the extent of modifying her identity. The passages where, refusing to recognize her pregnancy, she rationalizes her body's sensations are ironic because the experiences they describe are typical, although unexplored in previous fiction. Thus a major component of the novel's appeal is to ironic recognition. Her body seems to be following an agenda of its own, her flesh lying uncomfortably on her bones, burning and "unaccountably" (323) swelling. This image is the negative side of the natural unity of the veld, which Martha felt as a melding of her own body with rivers and trees. One morning when she is very nauseated, "the suspicion she had been ignoring for so long became a certainty" (358). Martha is profoundly divided. Although she feels the web tightening round her, she is also "most irrationally elated" (359), her body subject to its own reasons and emotions. She is caught up in "an immense impersonal tide" (361), along with all the other women whose pregnancies reflect an increased wartime birthrate. She is disturbed by the idea that all rational thought is useless against the conspiracy a woman joins in against herself: "what was the use of thinking, of planning, if emotions one did not recognize at all worked their way against you?" (363). Her entire pregnancy illustrates both the loss of individuality in the workings of biological forces and the exhilaration that can come from submitting to them.

The imperatives of biological and social roles operate in similar ways to undercut individual identity. The impersonal and irresistible force sweeping over Martha is paralleled by the "rising tide of [war] excitement . . . like a poison" (326) that all the young men, wanting to "be swallowed up in something larger than themselves" (327), aggressively welcome. Unlike Martha's biological imperative, the war excitement is a function of the collective, deliberately invoked by official activity such as Sister Doll's Red Cross course and furthered by the nostalgia that prompts the Sports Club orchestra to play the songs from the First World War. Martha, under the influence of this war fever, feels even more incapable of shaking off her private fears: when she realizes that the women of her mother's generation each have a dead man in their past because of the First World War, she succumbs to the fear of the "great bourgeois monster, the nightmare *repetition*" (337).

At the same time that Martha becomes caught up in the "great central drama" (373) of pregnancy, imagining the process of evolution that the fetus is reenacting, she is also conscious of Freudian repetition, wondering if her mother-in-law, whom she will soon meet, is a "forecast of her own fate" (376). With comic logic she thinks that, if Mrs. Knowell does not resemble Mrs. Quest, "in its own malevolent way, fate would adjust this incompatibility too, and naturally to Martha's disadvantage" (376). She feels divided against herself, one part caught in "the impersonal blind urges of creation" while her mind "like a lighthouse" (387) makes plans for the glorious time after she is delivered. Her mother of course demands that Martha, who tries to keep from being submerged by "the dark blind sea [of] motherhood," must "sacrifice herself to her children as she had done" (387).

Martha feels cut off from her roots when the Quests leave the farm; the balance between the veld and the city has been overturned. However, the mystical integration with nature brought on by her visionary experience on the veld is replayed in a physical reprise: in a torrential rain she goes with a pregnant friend to sneak a look at the nursing home where they have both reserved beds for their deliveries. On the way home they rip off their clothes and sit in a pothole full of muddy water teeming with frog spawn, frogs, snakes—all forms of life for which, like "the crouching infant . . . moving tentatively around its prison" (395), water is the natural element. This experience eases Martha's soul by integrating her and her unborn baby into the wholeness of the veld.

While men too are caught in their own kind of "terrible necessity" (440), Lessing, opposed on principle to war as she has never been to motherhood, is less sympathetic, more ironic, about their predicament. Douglas, sent home before he gets to the front, feels that he has been expelled from the one collective that would have provided the climax of his life, "real experience at last" (483). His first night home Martha sees the ferris wheel again and, terrified she might conceive a second time, succumbs again to the old trapped feeling. Although she is not pregnant, the house in the suburbs Douglas finds a way to finance traps her almost as effectively. She enters another new collective, the community of suburban women, whose contriving, scrimping, and scraping underwrite their enormous houses with four or five servants, new appliances on the hire purchase, and extravagant life insurance policies. When Douglas jokes that he will hide her contraceptive, she

## CHILDREN OF VIOLENCE

begins to long for the "dryness, barrenness, stunted growth" of the high veld (514).

Martha, whose analytical powers are increasing, foresees for herself the kind of repetition that overtook the unaware Mary Turner. In her mother Martha sees precisely the person she does not want to become. A teasing remark from Douglas that at Mrs. Quest's age she will be just as bad is enough to activate her deepest terrors: "if she had remained in the colony when she wanted to leave it, got married when she wanted to be free and adventurous, always did the contrary to what she wanted most, it followed that there was no reason why at fifty she should not be another such woman as Mrs. Quest, narrow, conventional, intolerant, insensitive" (294). A scene in which Mrs. Quest, observing that Martha looks pregnant, seizes the opportunity to bully her, shows the mechanism underlying the relationship between them. Although Martha is perpetually irritated by her mother's "need to lead every other life but her own" (354–54), she persuades herself that, disappointed in her life as Mrs. Quest is, her behavior is "natural, . . . even harmless and pathetic" (353). Filled with a crippling pity, she reflects that, as the necessity of repetition binds them both, Mrs. Quest cannot help behaving as she does.

Martha understands that Mrs. Quest is only one example of a historical type when she discovers that all the young couples in the suburban community have "one or two mothers-in-law dependent on them for emotional satisfaction, pathetic middle-aged women left high and dry by society with nothing to do" (515); nonetheless she finds devastating Mrs. Quest's vicious criticisms that come "welling from some deep crack in her nature" (515). It seems that Mrs. Quest who, like Douglas, wants to dominate Martha, can feel competent only if she triumphantly exposes what she considers Martha's faults; that same "deep crack in her nature" makes her leave her possessions—coats, cardigans, powder bowls—littered over Martha's home, which Martha, who makes excuses for her mother even when angry, regards with a "tired pity which was the greatest degree of charity she could achieve" (519). Her mother turns into a little girl when Martha tries to reason with her, just as Douglas becomes a "sulky little boy" (524) when she does not comply with his wishes. In fact, both Douglas and Mrs. Quest have the same end in view, that each will direct Martha's life, and their ideas of what it should be seem very similar. Their unacknowledged collusion becomes apparent when Mrs. Quest refuses to help Martha escape from Douglas's violence.

World War Two educates Martha into a world larger than family, neighborhood, even the Sports Club or the Left Book Club can provide. It stimulates, for instance, a discussion of the relations between whites and native Africans. It is officially decided that the blacks should not be conscripted; if armed, they might

## *CHILDREN OF VIOLENCE*

rise against the whites. The analysis of the British class structure begun in *The Grass Is Singing* is developed further when Martha for the first time meets white soldiers from the ranks. All the young whites from the colonies are regarded as officer material because of lifetime of ordering the blacks about has "accustomed [them] to positions of authority" (344). When the "groundlings," the support personnel, arrive on the local Royal Air Force base, a new kind of man appears: a working-class white who, seeing the short supply of white women, happily goes to the coloured section, to the general horror of the Zambesians. In a leftist group Martha works alongside these men from Britain, some of whom are committed communists. Their attitudes are very different from those of the colonials, who are all more or less middle class. Since the German invasion in 1941, which invalidated the Nazi-Soviet Pact of 1939 and pushed Russia into the Allied camp, the collective attitudes toward Russia have changed, the troops becoming "heroes and magnificent fighters" (537). In communism Martha catches sight of a "glorious outline of a view of life she had not suspected" (545), her enthusiasm for which is of the same kind as her feeling for her visionary city: "For the first time in her life, she had been offered an ideal to live for" (546). Her habits of mind, seeing the works of fate, of inevitability, of necessity everywhere, welcome the logic of history as a compelling idea. Communism also offers the abolition of the family and thus an end to the cycle of repetition: the Mrs. Quests and

### UNDERSTANDING DORIS LESSING

Mrs. Knowells—those pathetic middle-aged women with nothing better to do than run their children's lives or efface themselves completely out of the fear of doing so—will be given other ways to live in the new society. Communism, based on the future rather than the past, on the working class rather than the bourgeoisie, offers a solution for the problems of family relations as well as race relations. And, it goes without saying, it will put an end to the second-class status of women.

While communism seems to promise a way out of the entrapment of her marriage, ironically enough a man is the vehicle through which Martha joins the leftist movement. She falls in love not only with the revolution but also with a comrade, an upper-class Englishman with labor movement affiliations posted to the colony with the Royal Air Force. She discovers that no one believes her intention to leave Douglas comes from political conviction. Older women urge her to stay with him because Caroline needs her biological mother, because men can't help the way they are, or because they themselves sacrificed to keep their families together. Essentially it is the reason that Mrs. Knowell articulates: "her own life was made to look null and meaningless because Martha would not submit to what women always had submitted to" (596). The only person who seems to understand Martha is, ironically, Caroline, with whom she has a deep bond of "sympathy and understanding" (599). Martha's last words to Caroline are that she is setting her free—free from the tyranny of repetition. Judge Maynard, who officiated at Martha's wedding, capsulizes Martha's position: "with the French Revolution for a father and the Russian Revolution for a mother, you can very well dispense with a family" (605).

### *A Ripple from the Storm*
### (1958; covering the years 1941–43)

Between *A Proper Marriage* and *A Ripple from the Storm*, Lessing wrote *Retreat to Innocence*—a book she found so unsatisfactory she has never allowed a reprint—which outlines the opposition between the private life and the public life in a more schematic way than it assumes in *Children of Violence*. Set in the London of the early 50s, it tells the story of the love affair between an older man, a Czech refugee whose entire life has been politics, and a young woman who, reacting to the nastiness of World War Two, insists on the false innocence of a bygone domestic ideal, a type prevalent during the 50s. This novel again reveals Lessing's prompt awareness of historical attitudes and character types.

The dialogue that in *Retreat to Innocence* was neatly divided between two characters is internalized in Martha. In *A Ripple from the Storm* she is still trying to find a balance between public and private, outer and inner. Although she has dismissed the roles provided by marriage and motherhood as useless in her quest for identity, she still believes she will be able to form one from some other role. The collective ideal of romantic love has such a grip on her imagination that even when she discovers that William, the man for whom she supposedly left Douglas, is unimportant, she still longs for "a close complete intimacy with a man."[9] When William goes away, she understands that she has an empty space beside her, waiting for a new man who will allow her "to be her 'self'—but a new self, since it is his conception which forms her" (48).

Pernicious though this ideal of romantic love may be, the collective of communism is actually more threatening to the balance between inner and outer because it addresses the deepest needs of Martha's nature, providing a romance more fervent than any of her sexual relationships. As Mrs. Van says in *Landlocked*, "You communists . . . are romantics, every one." Martha feels part of the "great band of international brothers," trustworthy and devoted; it is in the service of the communist group that she develops into the reliable, competent person she will be for the rest of her life. Her romantic picture of the Soviet Union assures her that "it's all finished, race prejudice and anti-Semitism" (31). Her vision echoes her image of the four-gated city, a vision shared by Jasmine Cohen, cousin to the Cohen brothers and indefatigable party worker. Martha is so engaged that her analytical faculties are skewed: when Solly Cohen, now a Trotskyite, tells her that Stalin has

## *CHILDREN OF VIOLENCE*

executed Red Army officers, she accuses him of being corrupted by the capitalist press.

Her analytical faculties, however, still work on what she herself observes. Just as she has analyzed the dynamics of the family and of the social group as represented by the Sports Club, she scrutinizes the dynamics of the political group, where her romantic ideas about communism are put to the test. The local RAF camp contributes a number of comrades, who begin to make invidious comparisons between the working class and the middle class, always to the advantage of the former, using them to belittle the women of the group when their indiscriminate marriage proposals are turned down: they reject spoiled colonial women in favor of the "coloureds" who, like British working-class women, "know . . . how to suffer" (108). This group, ostensibly putting aside personal matters for the sake of the revolution, is as rife with pride, ambition, desire to control, and need to be served as any collective Martha has joined.

Martha's involvement with communism leads to a serious psychological imbalance, which is brought to her attention through dreams, in Jungian thought an avenue from the unconscious, that becomes increasingly important to her. She is so busy with her outer, collective life that her inner, individual life disappears from conscious consideration. Her unconscious mind attempts to restore the balance, engineering a spell of illness, which is the only time she can be alone. In a fever she has a two-part dream that frightens her not because of the manifest content but because of the lack of connection between the two parts—an image of her psychological state. Both—a nostalgic dream of England, followed by one of a monstrous dinosaur embedded in the layered rock of the veld—seem, as Rubenstein points out in the latter case, to be connected with May Quest.[10] The atmosphere of the first part shows that it expresses a longing to escape; the second, a perverse version of the veld image, emphasizes in the fact that the dinosaur is still alive the atavistic desire for integration into a whole that, ignoring individuality, insists on the inevitability of the repetition from which Martha must escape. Thus while the conscious mind is occupied with the outer life, the unconscious carries on through symbols the dialogue between inner and outer.

In spite of Martha's clear insight into the comrades, her political idealism reinforces her feminine compliance; together they lead her into another constricting marriage that does nothing to call a new self into being. Anton Hesse, a seasoned communist, refugee from Hitler's Germany, takes over Martha by the simple expedient of caring for her while she is sick, thus signaling to the group that they are a couple. Once more Lessing breaks new ground in her description of women's sexual experience: when Martha and Anton begin to make love, Martha realizes that he is a hopelessly premature ejaculator. Nevertheless she submits to his moral blackmail: when he tells her he is in some danger of being returned to an internment camp because of his affair with her, a young British woman, she agrees to marry him. Then she sees an aspect of him unnoticed in the efficient comrade: "dependence, something almost childlike" (185). As soon as the ceremony is over, she realizes that he is as concerned about furniture as any suburbanite. Although she manages for some time to maintain her respect for the dedicated communist, she knows that she has once more drifted into an intolerable situation. When she realizes that he wants her to be more of a wife, less of a communist, she begins to despise him. In his demands that she fulfill the conventional feminine role he is every bit as insistent as Douglas.

The compliance leading to Martha's marriage to Anton is echoed by a paralysis of the will toward her mother, who harasses Martha when she is sick and mentions Caroline, the "poor little girl" (100), at every opportunity. As the guilty party Martha has relinquished all maternal rights and meekly accepts all Mrs. Quest's assaults. However, her repressed maternal guilt comes out in her spirited support of her friend Maisie Gale's right to keep her illegitimate child in the face of the Maynards' grandparental attempt to gain custody.

Anton's attitudes are alarmingly reminiscent of nature's devaluation of the individual, which underlines the superiority of Martha's vision of the city in the veld to the communist ideal. He despises the various items of "welfare work" undertaken by some of the group—Andrew McGrew, for example, marries Maisie because she is pregnant and Binkie Maynard, the baby's father, is at the front. He objects when members suggest cordial relations with the native population, pointing out not only that the historical moment is not right for such activity, but also that such decisions must be made on analysis rather than on feeling. He is in fact invalidating the individual response by insisting on the primacy of the collective. In this respect he is much like Judge Maynard, who is the opposing political pole of the novel; both intellectuals and authority figures, the one represents the present, the other the projected future.

While Anton's group has a certain success, infiltrating various leftist causes such as the Progressive Club and the Sympathizers of Russia and being co-opted onto the executive board of the Labour Party, it ultimately collapses, not because of governmental interdict—though Judge Maynard has exerted himself to get some of the British airmen posted elsewhere—nor even because of overwork, but essentially because of the strains that Anton's way of running the group entails. The implicit comparison between Anton and Athen Gouliamis, a dedicated communist and a humanist, is all in Athen's favor: he is a touchstone of what a human being should be.

Martha's paralysis of will becomes an image of the political collective as well as of her psychological state. She is overwhelmed by the sense of futility arising from contradictory perceptions that what had happened to the group was inevitable, yet at the same time "unreal, grotesque, and irrelevant" (271). The group's collapse has cut her off "from everything that had fed her imagination." She begins to despair of ever finding her real self: "I'm not a person at all, I'm nothing yet—perhaps I never will be" (270). She slides into sleep "like a diver weighted with lead" (272). In both her private and public lives she has reached a stopping place on her developmental journey.

### *Landlocked* (1965; covering the years 1944–49)

Before writing *Landlocked*, Lessing became interested in Sufism, a form of mysticism without a well-defined set of tenets, official organization, or priestly hierarchy, which centers on the individual's search for spiritual enlightenment through the experiences of ordinary life. In *Landlocked* Lessing explicitly invokes the Sufi teaching story, a kind of fable susceptible to interpretation on many different levels, by using examples as epigraphs. Because, as Lessing points out, Sufism articulates what she has always believed,[11] there is no philosophical disjunction between the earlier and later volumes of *Children of Violence;* Martha's adolescent mystical experiences on the veld are consonant with a Sufi world view.[12] The earlier volumes stress Martha's spiritual growth through separation from constricting collectives such as the family, motherhood, political parties, group minds of all kinds, which demand the loss of identity in roles, leading to what the Sufis call the false self. The last volume stresses her search for her true self through spiritual evolution, an exercise the Sufis believe will lead to evolutionary growth, both psychological and physical, for all humanity; as an epigraph to part 4 of *The Four-Gated City* explains, "Sufis believe that . . . humanity is evolving towards a certain destiny. We are all taking part in that evolution. Organs come into being as a result of a need for specific organs." *Landlocked* documents Martha's change in direction from an outward to an inward search for her true self.

Martha suffers from self-division, a condition *The Golden Notebook,* written between *Ripple* and *Landlocked,* thoroughly explores as it develops in great detail the connection between breakdown in the individual and the collective. *Landlocked* deals with a similar situation but with a more optimistic outcome, at least for Martha as an individual. Dreams again provide her with an image of her situation: she is a "large house . . . with half a dozen different rooms in it" which have to be kept separate.[13] The center lit space is uninhabited; she tries to imagine who will occupy it, testing out the men she has been attracted to in the past, such as the Cohen brothers and Athen Gouliamis. But because she knows she is waiting "for a man . . . who would unify her elements . . . like a roof, or like a fire burning in the centre

## CHILDREN OF VIOLENCE

of the empty space" (302), she is careful to avoid those who, like Solly, have the capacity for only a superficial relationship.

The man to unify her elements soon enters her life. Thomas Stern, a Polish Jew who emigrated before the Nazi purges wiped out his entire family, helps actualize much of Martha's dormant potential. The circumstances in which he first appears dramatize his personality without making him the center of the scene. With several leftist friends Martha watches a newsreel showing the German armies in retreat (a foreshadowing of the nuclear holocaust in the appendix to *The Four-Gated City*). Although Martha and her comrades have been violently anti-Nazi, when confronted by the suffering individuals rather than the threatening collective they with one exception are aware of the pathos of "defeated men, men in the last extremity of hunger, cold and defeat, thousands and thousands of hollow-cheeked ghosts, a ghost army, their feet in rags, rags binding hands, shoulders, heads, bits of cloth fluttering in the cold cold wind of that frigid spring" (320–21). But Thomas Stern, devastated by a firsthand account of the liberation of Bergen-Belsen (the first concentration camp opened by the Allies), says he would "torture every one of them myself, with my own hands" (323). The Jews' fate at the hands of the Nazis has psychologically damaged Thomas.

Martha understands the danger of a relationship with such a man: on Victory in Europe Day, when emotions are running high in the colony (as they were in all British colonies, in Britain, Europe, Russia, and the United States), she sees that Thomas is "sucking her into an intensity of feeling" (353) more serious than anything she has ever felt or, indeed, will ever feel again. Nonetheless her relationship with Thomas ends her self-division. Thomas, appropriately a nurseryman, puts her back in touch with the veld, his real home. Driving to his farm Martha has a visionary experience. The spaciousness of the veld stimulates a matching image inside her; she sees in it people as tiny figures against a backdrop of time and space, which in Lessing's world view as developed in the *Canopus in Argos* series seem to be linked to the evolution of the human species. Thomas's old teacher emphasizes this connection: "the next thing for man [is] to feel the stars and their times and their spaces" (460). Thomas has touched her imagination, as Lynda will in *The Four-Gated City*, so that she senses the whole in a more coherent way. Her sense of herself in time, as part of the historical development of the human race in relation to the larger world of the universe, becomes as real to her as her place in nature did on the veld. Through Thomas, Martha feels attached to the human race past, present, and future.

Thomas stands at the intersection of the most personal and the most general; in him the private and the historical meet. In the description of Martha's and Thomas's relationship Lessing uses an extraordinary image to capture the innate connection between the private and the public, the individual and the collective: "Perhaps, when Thomas and she touched each other, in the touch cried out the murdered flesh of the millions of Europe—the squandered flesh was having its revenge" (428). She becomes aware that the impersonal forces entering her with her love for Thomas are similar to those of pregnancy, for once again "her body had become a newly discovered country with laws of its own" (368). She understands the magnitude of their effect on her; they had "made such changes in her . . . that now she was changed and did not understand herself" (482). As the Sufis believe, the most ordinary experience, which surely includes sexual activity, can provide a path to enlightenment.

The volatility of life distresses Thomas, a man who grew up expecting the kind of stability conferred by being born, marrying, dying, and being buried in the shade of the elm tree one's grandfather planted; even though no one lives like that any more, everyone's emotions are still geared to the pattern. This expectation of intergenerational permanence is represented in *The Four-Gated City* by the Coldridge family house, which turns out to be as ephemeral as life under the patriarchal elm. Thomas is a tormented soul, with the "eye of an insane artist" (371) and a split personality reminiscent of Dr. Kroll in "The Eye of God in Paradise." Feeling violence and death in his nerves and bones, he uses words like *mad*, *insane*, *maniac* in reference to himself.

His boundaries and Martha's become permeable during "the long process of breaking-down—as they both learned to put it—for the other" (482). This breaking-down—a form of dialogue—is possible not in spite of Thomas's incipient madness but because of it, as the fuller exploration of the idea in *The Golden Notebook* makes clear. From it comes Martha's expanding imagination, her fuller openness and consequent capacity for learning unconventional kinds of knowledge, as she does from the mad Lynda in *The Four-Gated City;* in fact, not until she encounters under Lynda's example what she comes to call "the self-hater" does she understand why Thomas went mad and died in the bush. Thomas projects his self-hate onto Sergeant Tressel, who oppressed the native soldiers under his command not out of cruelty but "out of carelessness, of sheer indifference" (409). Everything in life that distresses Thomas accrues to the image of Sergeant Tressel; he becomes Thomas's dark side, what Jung calls the shadow, a repository for all the unacknowledged evils of the self. Martha understands that what Tressel represents will eventually take Thomas away: "a red-faced fattish man in a badly cut dinner suit . . . was an enemy too strong for her" (415).

Martha's dream of imprisonment on a "high dry place while ships sailed away in all directions, leaving her behind" (466) reflects the sterility of both her personal life and her political life. The Africans, whose oppression first drew her into political activity, have dropped away from socialist organizations, whether Labour or communist and, rather than furthering the cause of international revolution, pursue nationalist goals. Suspicious of their white sympathizers, whose open help would in any case bring the charge of communism, they organize their own strike, the success of which demonstrates that as far as the Africans are concerned Martha's communist group has outlived its usefulness. Martha, disillusioned with political activity, understands she will never find her true self through a collective role.

At the end of *Landlocked* motherhood is the only collective role that Martha has left hanging. She has worked through other collectives, marriage and communism, for example, but she still believes she has managed to avoid dealing with the collective of motherhood. The cause of her avoidance is her unresolved difficulty with her own mother. Martha herself recognizes that her response to May Quest underlies problems in other relationships: Anton as well as Douglas resembles her mother in significant ways, which Martha realizes when a conflict with Anton reminds her of her arguments with her mother: "She [too] is always in the right" (329).

The relationship that Mrs. Quest has influenced the most is Martha's with Caroline. Not only has Martha been obsessed by saving her daughter from the "nightmare repetition," but she has had to endure Mrs. Quest's using Caroline as a weapon against her. Mrs.

Quest, who enjoys grandparental privileges even though Martha herself has no visitation rights, always calls Martha to tell her when Caroline visits. Martha never says "what her appalled, offended heart" (284) feels—that her mother enjoys punishing her. She accepts that "the essence of [her] relationship with her mother must be, must, apparently, forever be that Mrs. Quest 'couldn't help it'" (284). On one such visit she overhears Mrs. Quest speaking to Caroline with "the ease of love" (310) and wonders whether her mother ever liked her enough as a child to speak to her in that tone of voice.

The unresolved difficulties of her relationship with her mother surface both overtly and through the interventions of the unconscious. Martha begins to suspect that leaving Caroline might have been misguided but doesn't articulate this perception until *The Four-Gated City*. Coming face to face with the eight-year-old Caroline, who clearly suspects that Martha is her mother, she wonders what she could have been thinking of when she imagined "one day she'll thank me for setting her free. . . . Yet leaving the child it had been her strongest emotion: I'm setting Caroline free" (503). However, she has inadvertently consigned her daughter to the very situation she was obsessed not to repeat. She hoped to protect Caroline from the predatory claims of the previous generation, only to see them symbolized in the powerful image of a claw when she finds her father madly gripping Caroline's wrist with a hand that is "bone merely, a skeleton's hand with thin folds of flesh loose upon it" (499) and insisting that the child's hand belongs to him. It recalls the vigorous rapacity of T. S. Eliot's J. Alfred Prufrock: "I should have been a pair of ragged claws / Scuttling across the floors of silent seas."

Over the series there is an increasing sympathy for Mrs. Quest, which is further increased by a sequence from her point of view. A dream brings her a revelation: her own mother, beautiful but unkind, gives May three crimson roses that turn into a medicine bottle, symbolizing what Mrs. Quest knows very well, that her life has been all duty. On some level she associates the "cold, unfeeling" (346) Martha with this "cruel and mocking mother" (335). A scene in this section is written from both Mrs. Quest's and Martha's points of view so the thoughts and feelings of both, given equal weight, constitute a powerful dialogue. Although Martha has grown to understand "the brutal painfulness"(348) of her mother's life, she cannot allow herself to dwell on it. On her way to her father's sickroom, she thinks, "They'll do for me yet, between them, they'll get me yet if I don't watch out" by dragging her "down into this nightmare house" (348)—an image particularly threatening to a woman who has seen herself as a house without a center.

*Landlocked* marks the change in direction of Martha's search for the wholeness of her true self. The collapse of the revolutionary dream; the loss of Thomas who, trapped in his hatred of the shadow Sergeant Tressel, dies in the bush leaving only an eccentric manuscript overlaid with insane notes; and her suspicion that leaving Caroline has not been the success she had hoped have taught Martha that she must abandon the outward search and turn inward to the space she has discovered inside herself.

### *The Four-Gated City* (1969; covering the years 1950–97)

This novel again demonstrates Lessing's acute observation of political and social history. Its voluminous detail evokes the mood of the bleak 50s, which in Britain were characterized by the Cold War with the Soviet Union and the post-World War Two shortage of consumer goods, and of the swinging 60s, during which British popular culture, epitomized by the music of the Beatles and the fashions of Carnaby Street, swept the West, while expanding the consciousness through meditation and drugs was a popular concern on both sides of the Atlantic.[14] There is no better documentation of the cultural movements of these two decades anywhere in British literature.

The study of how power works in a class society, touched on in the previous volumes in the portraits of the Maynards, is further developed through the descriptions of the friends and acquaintances of the Coldridge family. The short-sightedness, self-seeking, and

## *CHILDREN OF VIOLENCE*

paranoia of such power—though not necessarily British power—is ultimately responsible for the accidental holocaust that, in the appendix, wipes out Europe as presently known.

*The Four-Gated City*, whose title is both ironic and optimistic, pulls together the thematic concerns and narrative strands introduced in the previous volumes of the sequence. But it does more than simply provide a resolution for what has gone before: taking "one step after another"[15] Martha develops a radically new position. When she loses her faith in communism, she also loses hope that organized politics of any persuasion can save the world or provide the circumstances for her self-development. The direction of Martha's growth is specified in an epigraph to part 4 as the attempt to develop through conscious evolution organs that will transcend time and space. Fulfilling a lifelong dream—oddly reminiscent of her mother's disappointed hopes—of emigrating to England, she finds the environment for such development in a group that looks suspiciously like a family, albeit an unorthodox one. The Coldridge household, based in the part of London where the Bloomsbury Group cultivated personal relations, provides a situation where Martha can develop her potential for new psychic skills and, perhaps as important for her individual integration, work through some roles she has been avoiding.

Free for the first time in her life from the claims of others, Martha continues to explore the nature of the self. Her freedom from roles prescribed by a collective sensitizes her to the fluidity of the personality, which she tests by wandering round London offering different names and false biographies to the people she meets. These encounters represent an extreme application of what she had already discovered in Zambesia, that different situations call diverse personalities into being, none of them, however, her true self. Because she is an outsider, she can move freely through the sharp class divisions, from the dockers in Iris's and Jimmy's café in South London to the fashionable lawyers in Baxter's in the West End.

Her loneliness and flexibility of the personality, combined with the self-imposed stress of eating and sleeping too little and walking long distances at night, make her "alive and light and aware" (35). She prizes this heightened consciousness characterized by a "soft dark receptive intelligence" (36). Her potential for this heightened consciousness was first drawn out by Thomas Stern, whose influence remains with her in spite of his descent into madness and death. With Jack, a man resembling Thomas in his attitudes toward time, sex, and death, she gains a kind of sexual communion that brings her a double visionary experience. The first, a version of her experience of wholeness on the veld, shows "a golden age" before the birth of consciousness, when the human family walked in unity with the animals; the second is a prophetic picture of herself as a middle-aged woman, "thickened and slowed" (60), in a

## *CHILDREN OF VIOLENCE*

London house full of children with tortured, hurt faces, which is to be fulfilled in her life with the Coldridges.

The problems of motherhood from the perspectives of both parent and child still haunt her. She confesses to Jack (who wants to impregnate all his girls and gather them under one roof in a perverse version of the Coldridge household as it ultimately develops) that she was mad to think leaving Caroline would free her daughter from the nightmare of repetition. Martha had accepted the communist analysis of the family as "a dreadful tyranny, a doomed institution, a kind of mechanism for destroying everyone" (67). Now she understands that the "mistake is, to think there is a way of not having to fight your way out" (68). Later, driven into psychoanalysis by the threat of a visit from Mrs. Quest, she understands that she did not resist her mother in the right way at the right time, confronting her with passive defiance rather than anger. While in the course of this novel she manages to play the nurturing role she refused with Caroline, she never succeeds in working out the relationship with her mother, even through a surrogate. The painful bond is broken only with Mrs. Quest's death. Although Martha herself never constructs a satisfactory daughter role, other Lessing characters continue the mother-daughter dialogue in *The Memoirs of a Survivor* and *The Diaries of Jane Somers* with more positive results.

Just as she drifted into marrying Douglas and Anton, so Martha gets sucked into a family constellation containing a mad wife and a nephew whose father has fled to Russia and whose mother, a refugee from the Holocaust, has gassed herself. "Tailor-made for me" (93), she cries ironically but, as Freud has amply demonstrated, utterances intended as jokes often conceal a significant truth. Unlike her two marriages, which added nothing to her self-development, Martha's involvement with the Coldridges enables her to play the role she has so far declined and the value of working through which she comes to recognize. Not only Paul, Mark's abandoned and orphaned nephew, but Francis, Mark's and Lynda's son, needs mothering. Eventually when their cousins, Gwen and Jill, reach adolescence, Martha, with a certain ironic distance, acts as surrogate mother to them as well. Further, she probes hidden psychological recesses in herself under the influence of Lynda, who is ill because she cannot cope with the collectively determined roles of Mark's wife and Francis's mother. This inability is one with which Martha sympathizes, for just as Martha herself escaped these roles into political activity, so Lynda has escaped into madness, which is very much part of the atmosphere of the household.

The madness of the household parallels the international situation, which steadily deteriorates. Mark collapses into breakdown under the social pressure consequent on his brother's defection to Russia; Martha feels that war between the West and the Soviet Union is approaching. As she can support neither, she plans

## *CHILDREN OF VIOLENCE*

to kill herself if war breaks out. The wartime alliance has given way to the Cold War; war has broken out in Korea; Senator Joseph McCarthy's Un-American Activities Committee is hunting down communists and ex-communists; the anticommunist hysteria in Britain is so great that the entire Coldridge family—including Arthur and Phoebe Coldridge, who are anticommunist members of the Labour Party—fear they might be sent to jail, leaving the children without caretakers. Everywhere the communists and the anticommunists become more rigidly adversarial. Martha alternately finds herself possessed by each extreme but recognizes that if she allows herself to succumb to the climate of hatred on either side, she will open the door to all kinds of violent feeling: "Shapes of hatred much larger than she could envisage waited like shadows on a nursery wall for fear to fill and move them" (194). Martha understands that she needs to attend to her psychological state, but she balks at the prospect of having to "untie knots of violent emotions" (194), a task she eventually undertakes with Lynda's help.

Abandoning the artificially constructed group based on ideology for one based on wholeness, Martha develops an organic process crucial to her future world view. When she contemplates the image of the house as a whole, she perceives that the people who live there, the madwoman in the basement, the two sad children, she and Mark, all constitute an organic whole, just as later, when the crisis approaches, Francis's commune

## UNDERSTANDING DORIS LESSING

forms because of the members' personal relationships. Working consciously on this image of wholeness, she manages to dispel thoughts of death. Although so much is going on in the house, Martha herself feels uninvolved, becalmed, dormant. "The ragged sycamore tree, thinned by the late autumn" (183) is an image of her condition, even though the tree itself is now showing spring green. She strives to evolve an image of the organicism of life, comparable to a plant, which grows in "a shape that is inevitable but known only to itself until it becomes visible" (192). Even in Bloomsbury she has visions recalling the unity of life on the veld and implying a larger wholeness: "The moon rose. Light came into the room and the tree's shadow dissolved. Over the earth's shoulder the moon was catching light from the sun. A quietness came into the room, with the vision of the little world, one half bathed in moonlight, the other in sunlight" (194). This view, observed from space like Anna Wulf's exercise of holding both the whole world and a single drop of water in her mind simultaneously, suggests a larger whole than the terrestrial unity of the veld.

A central scene makes explicit the parallel between the house and Martha's psyche, a correspondence echoing the image of Martha's psychological state as developed in *Landlocked*. Martha, walking through the house to announce supper, reflects that "there seems to be no centre . . . nothing to hold it together. . . . This was the condition of being a middle-aged person, a deputy in the centre of a house" (336). This lack of a center promotes a paralysis of will, which is accompanied by an inability to remember large areas of her life. The only significant thing she recalls from childhood is her vision of the city in the veld. She cannot remember rooms she has lived in with her husbands or specific details about Caroline, now a shadowy figure. The news of Mrs. Quest's imminent visit to London brings Martha to the edge of breakdown.

During this period of emotional distress Martha becomes much more aware of the silent watcher, the witness, the only part of herself that has been constant over the years. With a psychiatrist's help she understands that she is still torn by the conflicting emotions she felt toward her mother during her adolescence and young womanhood: "pity, strong, searing, unbearable [and] a wild need to run" (218). When she succeeds in remembering herself as a small child, she ends up in pain, crying, and a small black-haired girl, clearly her daughter Caroline (Martha herself is a tawny blonde), weeps with her: "Mama, mama, why are you so cold, so unkind, why did you never love me?" (221). This is Martha's first recognition that the very act of leaving by which she intended to free Caroline has in fact induced the nightmare repetition.

A lengthy section of *The Four-Gated City*, comparable to the one in *Landlocked*, is devoted to May Quest's point of view. She has been no more successful in participating in her son's life than in Martha's. That Mrs.

Quest's situation is not peculiar to her is underscored by the feelings of old school friends with whom she has corresponded for thirty years, whose difficulty with the present age is revealed as grief for their own loss of influence in the world: "how was it that overnight (so they felt) they had been transformed from people with responsibility and power into mendicants begging for the privilege of doing a granddaughter's shopping, or coaching a cousin's niece for their [sic] English O-levels?" (266)—a situation shared by those whose influence has been much greater, the Maynards, for example, who reappear in Martha's life when they pursue their granddaughter to London. Because for Martha the Maynards have always represented invincible authority, she can hardly believe how history has defeated them. To Mrs. Quest her loss of "responsibility and power" seems to be Martha's fault. Just before she returns to Zambesia she has a kind of catharsis, which dispels her crippling arthritis: "years and years and years of resentment [flooded out,] all focussed on Martha" (273). When less than a year later Mrs. Quest dies, Martha manages not to feel responsible—an advance from the guilt with which she has always responded to her mother.

Martha's last experience with Mrs. Quest helps Martha to see herself in the perspective of the entire life cycle: "Oneself . . . had to be, for as long as was necessary, screaming baby, sulking adolescent, then middle aged woman . . . reflected off the faceted mirror that

### *CHILDREN OF VIOLENCE*

was one's personality, that responded . . . every second, to these past selves, past voices, temporary visitors" (339–40). In her relations with the adolescent members of the household, she perceives that it is possible to speak past these temporary roles to the "permanent person" (340). She herself has become the matron, the figure whom in the opening scene of *Martha Quest* she most hated and feared. There is a certain irony in the fact that Martha, who tried to avoid such a role, has drifted into it in a social class that was always the object of her mother's aspirations.

Through her relationship with the Coldridge household, especially with Lynda, Martha develops a new skill, one showing the influence on Lessing of the Sufi belief in the evolutionary possibility of planned spiritual growth. As center of the house, Martha becomes attuned to the other inhabitants: she begins to "overhear" what some of them are thinking, as she did with Thomas. Mark is imploring Lynda to return to his room, Paul fantasizing revenge on those insufficiently appreciative of his talents. Since childhood Lynda has had this capability; in fact, her declaration that she could overhear her prospective stepmother's thoughts was the original reason for pronouncing her insane.

Hoping to learn more about what she suspects is collective-induced mental illness, Martha attends Lynda in her next relapse. This section includes acutely observed descriptions of disturbed behavior such as is usually seen only in clinical literature (an interest that

### UNDERSTANDING DORIS LESSING

Lessing pursued in her next novel, *Briefing for a Descent into Hell*): the most memorable is the image of Lynda moving slowly and deliberately round the walls of the basement, pressing and pushing as if to make them give. Following the traditional route to transcendental experience, Martha goes without food and sleep; once more she attains that "alert, clear state" (467) of her first weeks in London, in which she is subject to waves of emotion. She is swept by "great forces as impersonal as thunder or lightning or sunlight" (470), which are generally interpreted as love or hate or some other violent personal emotion. These forces are more examples of the kind of impersonal feelings she was overcome by during pregnancy, during the war fever of 1939, and during her affair with Thomas Stern. Encountering a sea of sound, she recognizes it as a function of what Jung calls the collective unconscious, which she can plug into like a radio or television set. In this state she meets an enemy, a hater, whom she realizes is not a personal figure but what Mother Sugar in *The Golden Notebook* names as a Jungian archetype, the destroyer motivated by joy in spite.

Because her disturbed state makes her more aware of the condition in others, she realizes there is no clear demarcation between the mad and the sane. Jimmy Wood, inventor of machines designed to control people in cruel and dehumanizing ways, is clearly not "all there," although he passes for sane amongst the general population (ironically, his wife goes to the asylum).

## *CHILDREN OF VIOLENCE*

Paul, like Jimmy, lacks a moral sense, although his basic generosity enables him to channel his talents into non-destructive behavior. Others, like Jack, Phoebe, Mark, and Francis, are unbalanced because of various obsessions promoted by their life experiences. Jack, surviving a naval disaster during World War Two, focuses all his energy on sex, which ultimately becomes destructive behavior; Mark and Francis both spend their lives looking after women who are incapable of returning their love; Phoebe Coldridge, who has maintained lifelong rigid control in the interests of serving the Labour Party, cannot recognize changes in historical circumstances, much less accommodate her behavior to them. Only Martha, by discarding the outworn roles of her false self, by working through those she had tried to avoid, and by consciously searching for her true self, manages to achieve a precarious integration.

The sensitivity Martha acquires during this process provides the bridge for Lessing's move into the space fiction of *Canopus in Argos,* which is clearly foreshadowed in *The Four-Gated City.* After a paradisal vision recalling the leaves, the earth, "the crystalline substance of the sky" (479) of the veld, she attains a sense of integration, feeling that the trees and clouds are "extensions of her and she of them" (480). Her joy is obliterated, however, by a view of human beings as "visitors from a space ship might see them" (481); the defamiliarized description of these "defectively evolved animals" is strongly reminiscent of the Yahoos of Jonathan

Swift's *Gulliver's Travels*. Martha's development of inner space thus points the way to Lessing's corresponding move, via *Briefing for a Descent into Hell*, to outer space in *Canopus*. Martha's second encounter with the self-hater makes her understand the duality of both individual and collective psychology: *"The tortured and the torturer. Am being both. . . . Hating . . . is the underside of all this lovely liberalism"* (510–11). This wavelength of hate is where Thomas Stern became trapped. The destructive propensity of the human psyche is hurtling to destruction not only individuals like Thomas Stern but the entire human race.

On the microcosmic level the dispersal of the Coldridge household when the Bloomsbury house is requisitioned by the local Council exemplifies the macrocosmic movement toward disintegration, the events constituting which take place very quickly, as though time itself were speeding up. This period is characterized by "a feverish transience"; Martha's life is "like a railway platform which served trains departing fast in every direction" (533). The younger generation of Coldridges takes to living in communes formed through personal contact rather than based on ideology. That the old political thinking is outmoded is demonstrated by Phoebe Coldridge, the authoritarian socialist, who considers their life style self-indulgent because society at large needs their talents. Francis, however, has a clearer understanding of what survival demands. Like Mark, who is beginning to build his city in the desert funded by

### *CHILDREN OF VIOLENCE*

American capital, he has a more accurate picture of the future. There is a persistent feeling that a catastrophe will shortly occur, the most specific manifestation of which is Lynda's dream of England poisoned.

For the first time since her early months in England, Martha is at loose ends, open and waiting. She summarizes what she has learned in her long *Bildung:* "one simply had to go on, take one step after another[;] this process in itself held the keys" (556). The novel proper ends with a paragraph emphasizing the unity of the human being with the natural world: the planet Earth, the river, the flowers, and the trees are intimately involved with Martha's perception that the next step in her personal evolution, as always, is immediately before her, "Here" (559).

This scene brings events up to the present of 1965—almost to the time of publication—when Martha has been in England for fifteen years. A remarkable appendix predicts the course of world events up to 1997, the last mentioned date. It moves away from Martha's consciousness to a larger view; her letter is only one document among many charting events after the catastrophe, which was apparently brought about by some kind of nuclear accident. Survivors are stranded in various places away from the main population centers; Martha herself is with a group on an island off the coast of Scotland. She helps raise a number of children, many of whom, having parapsychological capabilities, have taken a further step along the evolutionary path. By now Martha's talents for "hearing" and "seeing" are well developed, but some of the island children are born with these capabilities; Martha theorizes that eventually all human beings will be like them. In a letter to Francis Coldridge, now a rehabilitation administrator near Nairobi, she says, "People like you and me are a sort of experimental model and Nature has had enough of us" (608). She herself will die the following winter; Lynda Coldridge, however, is still alive, to be heard of again in *Shikasta*.

The future seems to belong to the Third World; certainly European-American imperialism has run its course. After the catastrophe the centers of power have shifted to Brazil, China, and to Africa, where Mark administers a camp for refugees in the place where he had hoped to build his city. The final document explains that a gifted child, significantly of mixed racial parentage, is to be sent from Martha's island to Francis in Nairobi as a gardener, presumably so that the need to incorporate nature into the city will not be forgotten. In spite of the devastation there must be some hope, a view to which Martha, still oriented toward the future, subscribes: "We took heart and held onto our belief in a future for our race" (604).

The ending of *The Four-Gated City* has been interpreted as either a prophetic statement or a warning about the world's future. Both of these extraliterary readings have something to be said for them. There are, however, literary reasons for such an ending. First, it is

### *CHILDREN OF VIOLENCE*

the logical culmination of a long sequence which needs to be definitively wound up. Following the advice of E. M. Forster, who over half a century ago pointed out the usefulness of death as a way to end a novel, Lessing killed off the civilization whose story she had been telling in order to escape from the "damned cage"[16] into which she had written herself. Second, the apocalyptic ending is implicit in the sequence's most important image. According to Revelation, the heavenly Jerusalem, the prototype of Martha's archetypal City, appears at the end of human history, after the world as presently constituted is destroyed (21.1–2). At the close of *The Four-Gated City*, the apocalypse has already arrived. Thus Lessing ends *Children of Violence* by making external and literal the scenario that began as internal and metaphoric in the consciousness of Martha Quest.

In doing so, she has demonstrated in fictional terms her concern with the writer's social responsibility. Mark, who forms with Martha what Sprague calls "collaborating doubles,"[17] bases *The City in the Desert* on the four-gated city of Martha's youthful day dream. Mark's book articulates so accurately the desires of its audience that numerous readers want to live in this city; a wealthy American is so inspired that he provides the capital for Mark to build it. Although Mark never abandons his dream of "that perfect city, a small exquisite city with gardens and fountains" (610), he ends his days administering the refugee camp on the land he bought for his ideal city. Thus Lessing symbolizes her contention that, life and art being inseparably entwined, writers must use their talents to benefit humanity by positively influencing the future.

## *Notes*

1. Lessing, "The Small Personal Voice," *A Small Personal Voice,* ed. Paul Schlueter (New York: Knopf, 1974) 14.

2. Mona Knapp points out that *Hesse,* the name Martha takes when she marries for the second time, refers to Herman Hesse, the author of a contemporary *Bildungsroman, The Glass Bead Game* (1943), translated into English in 1949; see Knapp, *Doris Lessing* (New York: Ungar, 1984) 39.

3. Lessing, *The Diaries of Jane Somers* (New York: Knopf, 1984) 148.

4. Lessing, *Martha Quest* (New York: Simon and Schuster, 1964) 21; subsequent references are noted in parentheses.

5. Mary Ann Singleton, *The City and the Veld: The Fiction of Doris Lessing* (Lewisburg, PA: Bucknell University Press, 1977) 19.

6. Singleton 20.

7. Roberta Rubenstein, *The Novelistic Vision of Doris Lessing: Breaking the Forms of Consciousness* (Urbana: University of Illinois Press, 1979) 35.

8. Lessing, *A Proper Marriage* (New York: Simon and Schuster, 1962) 286; subsequent references are noted in parentheses.

9. Lessing, *A Ripple from the Storm* (New York: Simon and Schuster, 1966) 48; subsequent references are noted in parentheses.

10. Rubenstein 59.

11. Knapp 13.

12. For a fuller explanation of the influences of Sufi thought on Lessing, see Nancy Shields Hardin, "Doris Lessing and the Sufi Way,"

## *CHILDREN OF VIOLENCE*

*Contemporary Literature* 14 (Autumn 1973): 565–82; rpt. *Doris Lessing: Critical Studies*, ed. Annis Pratt and L. S. Dembo (Madison: University of Wisconsin, 1974) 148–65.

13. Lessing, *Landlocked* (New York: Simon and Schuster, 1966) 286; subsequent references are noted in parentheses.

14. For a fuller description of 60s' attitudes to these ways of expanding the consciousness see Aldous Huxley, *The Doors of Perception* (New York: Harper, 1954) and Alan Watts, *The Joyous Cosmology* (New York: Random House, 1962).

15. Lessing, *The Four-Gated City* (New York: Knopf, 1969) 556; subsequent references are noted in parentheses.

16. Jonah Raskin, "Doris Lessing at Stony Brook: An Interview," *Small Personal Voice* 65.

17. Claire Sprague, *Rereading Doris Lessing* (Chapel Hill: University of North Carolina Press, 1987) 87.

# CHAPTER FOUR

# *The Golden Notebook* (1962; covering the years 1950–57)

Set in London in the 1950s, with long recollections of Rhodesia during World War Two, *The Golden Notebook* tells the story of a woman's breakdown, fragmentation, and healing into unity; it thus echoes the tenets of R. D. Laing's antipsychiatry, which hold that schizophrenia, a condition caused by "ontological insecurity"—Laing's version of existential anxiety—is a patient's way of coping with and ultimately healing the self-division forced upon the sensitive personality. As Draine puts it, the "book is about the terrors of destruction and stress of reconstruction."[2] However, it is not her story alone, for the chaos Anna Wulf slides into is both result and image of a general breakdown in Western society manifested in most of the individuals she meets.

In a statement echoing Anna's loss of faith in words as a trustworthy medium for conveying experience, Lessing says she wanted "to shape a book which would make its own comment, a wordless statement: to talk through the way it was shaped."[3] The chronological development of the traditional novel here gives way to an intricate structure in which *The Golden Notebook* is divided into five sections, each one including a segment of the "conventional novel" which is separated from the next by a segment from each of the four primary notebooks. These notebooks belong to Anna Freeman Wulf, the central character of "Free Women," the author of the best-selling novel *Frontiers of War*, who has determined to write no more fiction. Overwhelmed by a fear "of chaos, of formlessness—of breakdown" (23), she is suffering from an unacknowledged writer's block. She has begun to keep four notebooks rather than one because she thinks that compartmentalization will keep formlessness, which she equates with breakdown, at bay. When the notebooks peter out in response to "inner and outer" pressures, the new golden notebook is written not by Anna alone, but by Anna and Saul Green, an American with whom Anna shares a breakdown, a therapeutic *folie à deux;* in this notebook "you can no longer distinguish between what is Saul and what is Anna, and between them and the other people in [*The Golden Notebook*]" (24). Saul gives Anna the first sentence for "Free Women" (which is of course the first sentence of *The Golden Notebook*), the conventional novel Anna writes out of the raw material of the notebooks after the sequence of events described in the golden notebook has been completed. The fifth section of "Free Women" concludes *The Golden Notebook*.

Permeated by the philosophical positions in favor

during the 50s—socialist-realist theories of art, Freudian and Jungian psychoanalysis, existentialism, and Laing's antipsychiatry—*The Golden Notebook* deals with three major concerns of the mid-twentieth century: politics, madness, and what Lessing calls "the sex war" (25). These three concerns are equally involved in the social and psychological disintegration overtaking both Anna and the global community. They are kept in a unifying tension by the novel's emphasis on the act of writing itself, on the nature and responsibilities of the artist, the dialogue about which envelops all other topics in much the same way that "Free Women" envelops the notebooks.

In the introduction to the second edition of *The Golden Notebook*, Lessing specifies two overall themes, disintegration and unity. Disintegration—the threat of breakdown into chaos—is recorded directly in numerous instances throughout the notebooks, but the separation into notebooks itself symbolizes compartmentalization, the loss of unity. Similarly, what Lessing calls "the triumph of the second theme, . . . unity" (24) is expressed by the golden notebook, which comes into being when Anna abandons the primary notebooks. The dialogue between disintegration and unity that constitutes the subject of the novel also determines its structure. But the integrity of theme and technique does not end with the separation into notebooks; it extends to other formal elements such as the variety of "narrative forms—diary, letter, book review, parody, short story, film script, headline, news item, synopsis."[4] This inclusivity demonstrates the theme of unity.

Anna's name gives some insight into both the meaning and structure of the novel. *Wulf* clearly associates her with Virginia Woolf, with whom she shares a commitment to the act of writing, the need for a room to do it in, and a tendency to psychological breakdown; *Freeman* is obvious enough in its ironic juxtaposition to "Free Women." *Anna* perhaps recalls Anna Livia Plurabelle, the archetypal mother, the never-ending river of *Finnegans Wake*, whose circular structure, ending at the place where it began, is echoed in Saul's giving Anna near the end of the golden notebook the beginning sentence of "Free Women." Further, the plurality of Anna's selves is suggested by the last name of Joyce's protean character. This plurality consists not only of the many characters, so ably catalogued by Sprague,[5] who act as Anna's doubles, but also the various Anna functions— Anna-writer of the notebooks, Anna-character of "Free Women," and, as Joseph Hynes has suggested, Anna-editor of the entire *Golden Notebook* who, arranging the segments of "Free Women" and the primary notebooks around the golden notebook,[6] is responsible for both content and structure.[7]

For purposes of interpretation it makes sense to discuss the primary notebooks and "Free Women" separately, starting with the notebooks because Anna wrote them first. Each of the four deals with one aspect of Anna's experience that she now—beginning in 1950, the date of the earliest entry, to 1957, the date of the last—finds irreconcilable; she needs to isolate them from each other so that their contradictions and divisions will not destroy her. The threat of destruction manifests itself in various forms in each of the notebooks. The black notebook (the first entry of which is dated 1951 although it chronicles events of 1944; the last entry in Anna's handwriting is dated September 1956, although newspaper clippings continue through 1957) is devoted to her ongoing relations with *Frontiers of War*—which significantly resembles *The Grass Is Singing*, an example of Lessing's intertextuality—whose proceeds are continuing to support her. It records not only her transactions with film and television agents but also her attempts to reconstruct the experiences on which the novel was based. Dealing with the past, this notebook provides an overview of Europe in World War Two refracted through the colonial viewpoint. Anna concludes that *The Frontiers of War* was powered by a nostalgia for death and destruction—that this emotion, in fact, was the reason it became a best seller. She falls victim to cynicism, followed by despair that art, whether fiction or film, can ever record the truth of experience. The black notebook is largely an exploration of this artistic problem.

Dealing with the present, the red notebook (first entry 3 January 1950; newspaper clippings through 1957) records Anna's disillusionment with the British Communist Party, which reflects the moral collapse of the party itself as the news of Stalinist purges filters into Britain. The notebook includes various parodies and ironic stories centering on the naïveté of dedicated communists, and dwindles into newspaper clippings about such events as the electrocution of the Rosenbergs, the shelling of Quemoy and Matsu, and the testing of the hydrogen bomb. The end of Anna's hope for a better world through socialism results in a profound distress that seeps into all aspects of her life. Michael, Anna's comrade before he became her lover, appears first in this notebook.

The yellow notebook (undated) contains Anna's novel "The Shadow of the Third." Neither an endeavor to repossess the past nor to record the present, it is analysis through the hypothetical, an attempt "to set [Anna's] public and private selves into fictional perspective."[8] Ella, a fictional projection of Anna, represents contemporary woman as well, as her name, based on the French feminine pronoun *elle*, suggests. In transmuted form the events of "The Shadow of the Third" echo some aspects of Anna's experience. Ella, who works for a magazine catering to working-class women, writes a novel about a young man preparing to commit suicide; when with some surprise he understands his unarticulated intention, he kills himself. This novel reflects Ella's self-destructive tendencies, just as Ella's relations with her lover Paul parallel and exaggerate Anna's own dependency on Michael. At the same time, Paul is also another projection of Anna, serving as a vehicle for intellectual exploration just as Ella functions for Anna's emotional exploration. He introduces the idea of boulder-pushers who, in spite of their conviction that human stupidity cannot be overcome, like Albert Camus's existential hero Sisyphus still try to improve the human condition by patient labor at mundane tasks. Although Ella completes her novel, Anna never finishes "The Shadow of the Third"; disturbed by what it reveals about her own tendencies toward self-destruction and idealization of the other, she abandons the novel, and the yellow notebook winds down with a number of ideas for short stories related to events in Anna's life, recorded in the blue notebook and obligingly cross referenced so that the connection is not overlooked.

The blue notebook is more of a diary in the conventional sense, a book devoted to reportage. It covers the years 1950–57 (first entry dated 7 January 1950; last dated entry in Anna's handwriting September 1956), beginning seven years before the opening scene of "Free Women"; it includes her affiliation with the British Communist Party, her affair with Michael—the most intense love experience of her life—and her lengthy psychoanalysis with Mrs. Marks, the Jungian analyst with the Marxist name, which provides the basis for Anna's recovery when she has relived the therapy in her own experience. It also chronicles the confrontation between Saul and Anna, the experience that ultimately heals her of fragmentation, ironically enough by encouraging her to split into her numerous potential selves. Here she becomes aware that some selves come into being because they are drawn out by circumstances; the jealous lover, for example, is called into existence in the same way that her daughter Janet's presence brings out the concerned, efficient mother. Her relations with Saul make her realize that, like Martha Quest in *The Four-Gated City*, she has to go through madness before she can be healed of it. She is finally able to admit to having had a writer's block when she is on the verge of writing fiction again.

The conventional novel "Free Women" is both more inclusive and more schematic than any individual notebook because it presents the material from all of them in a more condensed and shapely form, heightening the pattern of cause and effect that the notebooks obscure by their wealth of detail. Further, characters and events may be modified for the same of meaning, as Anna confers blindness on Molly's son Tommy in order to increase his thematic significance. In the same way the portrait of Molly's ex-husband Richard, the tycoon, the enemy, both politically and in the sex war, of Anna and her friend Molly, rounds out the picture of British society. The description of international capitalism—an interest Lessing returns to in the description of the coffee cartel in *The Summer before the Dark*—balances the image of international communism appearing throughout *The Golden Notebook*.

Although considering each primary notebook and "Free Women" in isolation is necessary for seeing their overall patterns, this tactic admittedly obscures the forward movement of *The Golden Notebook*, falsifying the dialogic connections, which depend on juxtaposition, doubling of characters, and repetition of ideas. The major concerns of the sex war, politics, and madness cut across "Free Women" and all the notebooks, appearing in different guises and in different relations to each other. The subjects of protracted dialogue throughout the novel, they are components of the great themes of disintegration and unity, although they have neither watertight compartmentalization nor subordination in a defined hierarchy of ideas. Moving Anna's story forward, the arrangement of the various segments is by no means arbitrary. Each of the first four sections formed by one segment of "Free Women" is followed by one from each of the black, red, yellow, and blue notebooks (always in his order, chronologically through each notebook, though the entries from notebook to notebook may have been written on widely differing dates). Each section has a thematic coherence and a forward movement from disintegration to a new unity recognizing the existence of chaos, a unity characterized by process rather than stasis. This arrangement of the material undercuts the emphasis on linear time traditionally expected in narrative. However, it increases the reader's experience of felt life, which is never solely linear, much in the manner of *Finnegans Wake*.

## *THE GOLDEN NOTEBOOK*

### "Free Women" 1 (notebooks begin in 1951)

The first section of *The Golden Notebook* is by far the longest because it describes not only Anna's present situation but also, especially in the black notebook, the events leading up to it. The opening segment of "Free Women" begins in the summer of 1957, that is, immediately after the events of the golden notebook, in which Saul Green gives Anna the first sentence of "Free Women." The writing of "Free Women" is thus completely retrospective, undertaken after the pattern of events has become plain to Anna. It introduces all the themes and concerns that are developed at length in the notebooks; it also introduces all the characters or their doubles who appear there. It immediately announces the first theme of breakdown when Anna says to Molly, "As far as I can see, everything's cracking up."[9] This theme appears in the black notebook as the destruction of World War Two; in the red notebook as the beginning of Anna's disillusionment with communism; in the yellow as the breakup of Ella's relationship with Paul Tanner; in the blue as Anna's incipient psychological breakdown manifested in an inability to feel. It appears in a number of modalities, as suicide and a longing for death, specifically as nostalgia for the time of war, in the black notebook; in the red notebook it is echoed in Anna's reason for joining the Communist Party: "Somewhere at the back of my mind . . . was a need for wholeness, for an end to the split, divided, unsatisfactory way we all live" (142). It appears also as the fear of madness in the red notebook, where Michael is introduced as "a witch-doctor, a soul-curer" (142) and again when, canvassing in a working-class area for a communist candidate, Anna discovers that "this country's full of women going mad all by themselves" (146). It appears in the yellow notebook again as suicide, the subject of Ella's novel, through which death enters her life. This segment of the yellow notebook ends with Ella at the window night after night waiting for Paul to return, all the while thinking, "This is madness" (195). The theme has its most direct exposition in the blue notebook when Anna articulates her sense, which has been growing throughout this entire section, that everything happening in the world is death and destruction (202).

A persistent image of compartmentalization that runs through the entire *Golden Notebook* is especially evident in this section. The class structure of British society, which is, of course, a defense against social chaos, much as Anna's notebooks are a defense against the chaos of her life, is implicitly analyzed in "Free Women" in Anna's and Molly's interchanges with Richard and in their commitment to leftist politics, appearing overtly in such characters as the milkman, "one of those bloody working class tories" (15), whose son has won a scholarship that will guarantee him a place in the middle class. The first segment of the black notebook, which is ostensibly about Anna's best-seller, *The Frontiers of War*, includes a full discussion of class. Paul Brockenhurst, a Royal Air Force officer sent to Rhodesia to train as a pilot, is a self-proclaimed "member of a dying class" (72); the socialist views he espouses contrast ironically with his aristocratic attitudes. An uneasy tension exists between him and Ted Brown, an Oxford scholarship boy who, adoring and resenting Paul, does political missionary work among the airmen, motivated by his anguish that his opportunities are not available to all working-class youths. Ted Brown shows the kind of psychological fragmentation brought about by upward mobility that awaits clever working-class boys like the milkman's son in the first segment of "Free Women." This frame of mind is further elaborated in the yellow notebook when Paul Tanner, Ella's lover (a fictional double of Michael and, like him, a psychiatrist), manifests the emotional problems of social mobility; educated out of his class and natural responses, he suffers a "split in himself so painful that sometimes he wonders if it was worth it" (165).

The sex war occurs in "Free Women" as a battle between Anna and Molly on one side and Richard on the other when he demands their sympathy because Marion, his second wife, whom he has subjected to psychological abuse for years, has taken to drink. The relations between men and women presented in adversarial terms in "Free Women" are much more ambiguous in the notebooks. They are the subject of implicit and explicit dialogue, appearing in the relations among the characters, their actions, and their commentary. In the blue notebook Anna's attitudes are more flexible than in "Free Women" and certainly more open than Molly's. Anna's relations with Willi Rodde are strained because of sexual incompatibility, but she has a glorious night with Paul Brockenhurst, whose previous homosexual experience she does not condemn, any more than she condemns Maryrose's incest with her brother or George Hounslow's compulsive womanizing. However, Anna's fictional double, Ella of the yellow notebook, has very conventional views of the relations between men and women, preferring not to think when searching for happiness with a man. On the other hand Paul, also Anna's projection, observes that "the real revolution is, women against men" (184).

The topic of the life cycle—analyzed further in *Children of Violence*—appears in "Free Women" as a dialogue about parenting in the relations of all three adults with Tommy, the middle-class young man confused by the number of his opportunities. It is manifested in the black and blue notebooks as a subtopic of the relations between men and women: romantic mooning and sexual obsession mark the entry into puberty of June Boothby, the daughter of the landlord of the Mashopi Hotel, and Anna transcribes from an old diary the details of Janet's conception in 1944.

An important idea, upon which the progress of the novel depends, is a flexibility of the personality so extreme that people may be interchangeable: Anna notes that for both Richard and Marion, for instance, Anna seems to fulfill the same function as Molly. Molly herself enjoys playing various roles, while Anna is "always the same" (14)—a suggestion that Anna's rigidity may have something to do with her state of imminent breakdown. That personality boundaries are of some consequence is suggested by the fact that Anna allows Tommy to question her about her ideas and motives, almost as though he represents her conscience. Furthering the dialogue about the writer's responsibility, he points out that her decision not to write for a public audience while she "writes and writes in notebooks, saying what [she thinks] about life" (40) is irresponsible, arrogant, even contemptuous of others. This connection between them is strengthened by Tommy's observation that he too may become a writer.

The question of the role and responsibility of the artist, introduced in "Free Women" by the dialogue between Anna and Tommy, appears in all the notebooks. At the beginning of the black notebook it is presented indirectly through the description of the film industry's attempt to buy a book. Anna writes a synopsis of *Frontiers of War*, the satiric nature of which is not recognized by the agent until she points it out. Reflecting on her novel, Anna realizes that it was powered by nostalgia for the time of war in which the generation most directly affected—the men called to military service and the women who loved them—felt most fully alive. Ashamed of such "nihilism, . . . [this] longing to become part of dissolution"(62), Anna becomes cynical not only about the film industry that wants to capitalize on this negative emotion but about the act of writing itself.

Having been subject to a "twenty years preoccupation with this question of morality in art" (67–68) Anna focuses her major question on how well fiction tells the truth. She begins to doubt even her memory: "How do I know that what I 'remember' was what was important? What I remember was chosen by Anna, of twenty years ago. I don't know what this Anna of now would choose" (122). Her relation to her art has now reached a crisis point, as have all the other aspects of her life. The yellow notebook contains Anna's reflections on the way in which literature fails life: "analysis after the event" (196), it is untrue to the feeling of life as it was lived. What Ella lost during the five years she spent with Paul was *the power to create through naivety* (183). This observation clearly relates to Anna's disgust with the "lying nostalgia" of *Frontiers* that makes her unable to write.

The blue notebook immediately picks up the dialogue about the role of the artist. Leaving Tommy and Molly, Anna begins to write a short story but, deciding that fiction is an evasion, resolves to write down simply what happened. This process produces further information: for instance, Anna's husband, the father of Janet, is the Willi Rodde of the black notebook, although here his name is Max Wulf, a discrepancy that further confuses the boundaries between fiction and truth.

## *THE GOLDEN NOTEBOOK*

The psychotherapeutic management of breakdown appears in "Free Women" in Molly's and Anna's reminiscences of their therapy with Mrs. Marks, known as Mother Sugar because of "her tendency to sugar coat reality."[10] She provides the connection between psychotherapy and art in *The Golden Notebook*. In the blue notebook Anna uses Mrs. Marks as a touchstone against which to measure her own artistic experience. Mrs. Marks's therapy focuses on archetypal psychoanalysis; she urges Anna to associate every image and dream symbol with the primitive, with the unchanging aspects of the world and human nature. Thus, for her, art is stasis, an absolute, against which image Anna eventually formulates her own perception of art as a chaotic process dependent on historical circumstance and individual situation.

The end of this segment of the blue notebook pulls the first section together, providing a coda reiterating its overall movement. Breakdown is demonstrated as well as narrated in the way the diary collapses into clippings, resuming only to record Anna's dreams at the end of the four-year psychotherapy. At this point Anna has regained the ability to feel but registers only pain. A dream summarizes her condition, indicating through the image of a malicious miniature crocodile weeping frozen tears her guilt about profiting from the "lying nostalgia" of *Frontiers of War*, her ensuing cynicism about art, and her own frozen yet painful emotional state. The task that remains to her is to integrate a positive element into her vision of "joy in spite" (408), which has appeared to her in dreams as a Rumpelstiltskin figure, "an inhuman sort of dwarf" (214). In short, as Mrs. Marks helps her to understand, she must dream positively of destruction.

### "Free Women" 2 (dated entries in only the red and blue notebooks, August-September 1954)

This section chronicles Anna's attempts to pull herself out of the despair to which the death and destruction in all areas of her life have brought her. In the "Free Women" segment she explains to Tommy, in the spirit of the boulder-pusher, there's "another lurch forward" (234) on the path of human progress in spite of all the cruelty and ugliness. However, these attempts at an optimistic view do not convince: the image documenting their failure takes the form of a suicide attempt on the part of Tommy, who has been reading what he calls "madness books" (221).

A similar pessimism colors the dialogue about the relations between men and women. A simplistic view appears in "Free Women" when Marion complains about Richard's infidelity: "When he said he wanted to marry me, he said he loved me, he didn't say I'm going to give you three children and then I'm going off to the little tarts leaving you with the children" (239). Even though Anna tells her that she does not feel free and would in fact like to be married again, Marion persists in the conventional perception of Anna's life: "It's all very well for you, you live with just one child, and you can do exactly as you like" (239). Counteracting these simplistic views, Anna explores the complexities of the relations between men and women in the yellow notebook. Ella, to her surprise, realizes that she wants to go to bed with an American brain surgeon she met on a plane, discovering that she can proposition him even though only yesterday she thought that "women like me [have] emotions that don't fit our lives" (276). However, she cannot reach a climax, which leads her to theorize that "for women like me, integrity isn't chastity, it isn't fidelity, it isn't any of the old things. Integrity is the orgasm" (279). Here Anna follows the Freudian psychoanalyst Helene Deutsch, whose *Psychology of Women* (1944) was extremely influential during the 50s. Ella still feels the loss of Paul so strongly that she does not seem alive in any significant way. Anna carries these meditations one step further in the blue notebook, observing that "the disease of women in our time" (285) is impersonal resentment at injustice.

The black notebook contains a replay of Anna's experience with the film industry, this time with television. *Frontiers of War*, say one British and one American agent in almost identical phrasing, is "basically (just) a (very) simple love story" (245, 251). This interpretation omits all mention of the political issue of racism, the very element Anna considers the essence of the novel.

She greets the agents' suggestion to reduce *Frontiers of War* to a simple love story with ironic disgust while harboring a desire to retreat from the political herself. A parallel turning from the political to the personal occurs in Anna's own changing psychological focus when her hope of saving the world through socialism disintegrates, leaving her with only the wish for personal happiness. In the red notebook she records a dream about the world seen from space; colored like a map with the communist countries in a beautiful glowing red, it unravels into chaos. Waking, she puts her arms around Michael and retreats into a dream of happiness through romantic love, although through Ella she already knows on some level that Michael will leave.

In this section it becomes abundantly clear that Anna's loss of faith in art reflects a collective rather than an individual malaise. At a writers' meeting to discuss Stalin on linguistics, reported in the red notebook, she ruminates on the inadequacy of language itself in the face of the "density of . . . experience" (25). A naïve story about a British Communist Party member meeting Stalin illustrates the point: it is as much a parody as Anna's ironic synopsis of *The Frontiers of War*. In the blue notebook she records everything that happens to her in a single day in the hope that this technique will produce truth; she concludes that focusing equally on all details falsifies just as much as selecting details for fiction does.

## *THE GOLDEN NOTEBOOK*

Once again the blue notebook provides a summary of Anna's situation. She understands that she is about to leave the Party, which, because it marks a completed stage of her life, is a forward rather than a regressive movement: "And what next? I'm going out, willing it, into something new, and I've got to. I'm shedding a skin, or being born again" (302). Thus this section of *The Golden Notebook* ends with the possibility of positive change, even though it is the consequence of desperation.

### "Free Women" 3 (notebook segments dated 11 November, 1955 to December 1956)

This section shows Anna's fear of disintegration giving way to the possibility of unity through submitting to breakdown rather than resisting it with rigid and outworn structures. This view of mental illness as a therapeutic process leading to its own cure, widely promulgated by R. D. Laing in such books as *The Divided Self* (1960) and *The Politics of Experience* (1967),[11] underlies both content and structure: Anna finds it increasingly harder to maintain the compartmentalization of her notebooks; concerns and themes begin to merge and overlap.

This segment of "Free Women" dramatizes one way of maintaining sanity, which can be achieved by artificially limiting what one sees, as she herself has done in her relationship with Michael, for example. Tommy's failed suicide attempt leaves him blind but gives him control over his mother and everyone else coming into contact with him. His blindness gives him a congenial role that integrates his entire personality: "He's all in one piece for the first time in his life" (323). Rejecting such mutilation as a way to wholeness, Anna nonetheless understands that change must come into her life. She presents this insight as a dream: seeing that she is like a dry well, she dreams that she must cross the desert to reach the mountains. She tackles the problem again in the yellow notebook, which itself demonstrates the disintegration it describes. There is an increasing sense that breakdown—the cracking of a rigid mold—may lead to new awareness, new hope. "The Shadow of the Third" collapses into summary as Anna describes how Ella cracking holds on to the image of Ella "whole, healthy, and happy" (385). Failing in her attempt to force happiness, Ella accepts self-knowledge even if it entails unhappiness. Anna's way out of her despair is foreshadowed in the image of a "man and a woman ... both cracking up because of a deliberate attempt to transcend their own limits. And out of the chaos, a new kind of strength" (399–400).

Anna develops this insight further in the blue notebook. She remembers saying to Mother Sugar that people maintain their sanity by enforcing rigid limits on themselves; Tommy's blindness is Anna's metaphor for this generalization. In a session with Mother Sugar she has postulated the existence of a new kind of person: "there's a crack in that man's personality like a gap in a dam, and through that gap the future might pour in a different shape" (405). Further, she hypothesizes that people who are cracked may be keeping themselves open to new experience.

Anna's ruminations on the relations between men and women in "Free Women" reflect her increasing awareness of their complexity. Through Richard's real distress that Marion no longer has any time for him, she suggests that a man's love may be expressed in ways unrecognized by the women who know him, such as keeping his wife a kind of prisoner. Anna continues to explore these relations in the yellow notebook. When Ella becomes subject to a "raging sexual hunger . . . fed by all the emotional hungers of her life" (390), she is astonished because she has always assumed that a woman has no desire independent of a particular man. Ella's father believes that solitude is the only way to prevent men and women from being cannibals to each other; his experience with Ella's mother casts doubt on the impression created so far that only women can be victims in sexual relationships. The relaxation of the presumption that men are always to blame has its corollary in Anna's revelation in the black notebook: "I kept thinking stubbornly: Of course it's him, not me. For men

create these things, they create us. In the morning, remembering how I clung, how I always cling on to this, I
felt foolish. Because why should it be true?" (428). In short,
Anna rejects the idea that women are always victims.

In both black and yellow notebooks Anna continues
her dialogue about the artist's responsibility to the
truth. It seems that art is a scam not confined to those
who want to make money from it. The intellectual editors of the little magazines and the reviewers in Marxist
journals are just as biased as the makers of films and
television movies; the first, for example, may accept a
parody as the work of "the honest young artist with
built-in integrity" (375) or "Blood on the Banana
Leaves" as a real African story, while a Marxist review,
criticizing *Frontiers of War* because the situations and
characters are not typical, proclaims the need for "new
concrete forms of realism in the literature of Africa"
(381). Thus all media are more concerned to forward
their own agenda than to encourage artistic truth, the
achievement of which is admittedly difficult, if not impossible. After a year and a half of short entries in the
blue notebook, Anna concludes that this technique is
just as false as the fully detailed record of one day.

In this segment of the yellow notebook the relations
between Anna and her fictional double are clarified. Ella
is not Anna, rather an imaginary surrogate through
whom Anna explores the possible outcomes of certain
lines of action or the consequences of particular attitudes. Although Anna has said literature is analysis af-

ter the event, in this segment of the yellow notebook it is clear that she also believes literature may be hypothetical, involving both discovery and prediction. Ella thinks of a story about a woman who became exactly what her man wanted her to be—ruthless, treacherous, and promiscuous. She does not write it lest she turn into exactly that kind of woman.

In spite of her previous disillusionment Anna has great difficulty in finally renouncing her dream of a better world through socialism. The red notebook records a short-lived renewal of hope in the Communist Party. Although she has left the party, in November 1955 Anna has begun to attend meetings, infected by the hope for a "genuinely democratic" (382) party now Stalin is dead. In August 1956 Anna records her astonishment that less than a year previously she believed a new party possible; she begins to think that "the one form of experience people are incapable of learning from is political experience" (384).

The blue notebook reinforces the sense that Anna is about to undergo some important change. She has a recurrence of the dream about "joy in spite" (408). Although Mother Sugar has suggested that this force has positive as well as negative qualities, Anna is horrified when she recognizes it in a man reappearing in her life. At the same time she feels that something new is about to happen. This sequence of events foreshadows the appearance of Saul Green.

**"Free Women" 4 (the notebooks contain newspaper clippings for 1955–57; one dated entry for September 1956 in Anna's handwriting; no other dates]**

This section chronicles Anna's acceptance of her incipient breakdown, her willingness to work through her madness. Once more in "Free Women" she explores the situation through Tommy's experience. Marion, his stepmother, begins to stay overnight with Tommy in Molly's flat; it becomes clear that she has in essence left Richard for Tommy without ever stating such an intention. The oddly assorted pair—an image of one kind of breakdown—demonstrate on behalf of the "poor Africans" (438; Marion's words), the very population exploited by Richard's international financial interests. Talking to them at Richard's request, Anna understands that they are in a hysterical state; she feels unsure not merely of what she is going to say but "who the person is who will say it" (439); in short, she is very aware of the provisionality and permeability of personality. When she begins to talk about Tom Mathlong, an African activist, she suspects that she has "gone right over into Marion's and Tommy's hysteria" (440). Suddenly she mentions the mad Charlie Themba, who has recently cracked up, and understands that she has been leading up to this subject without being aware of her intentions. Her identification with Themba is clear from the repetition of the crocodile image that has appeared in a dream of her own. Her description of the claims of motherhood, however, signals her intention to limit her breakdown. Seeing Janet asleep restores her emotionally and gives her strength just as Tommy, her surrogate child, has drained her.

In this section the notebooks, which have been Anna's defense against disintegration, begin to collapse into each other. One after another they end in double black lines as Anna realizes they are not serving their purpose. Both the black and red notebooks are largely composed of newspaper clippings, which are only described, not shown. Those in the black notebook (from the years 1955, 1956, 1957) are about "violence, death, rioting, hatred, in some part of Africa" (449); in the red (1956 and 1957), about violence in Europe, the Soviet Union, the United States, and China. In the red notebook clippings Anna has underlined the word *freedom* every time it occurs—676 times. Each of these two notebooks contains a single entry in Anna's writing. The one in the black describes a dream about a television film being made from Anna's African experiences. She is appalled to see that what is being filmed is not what she remembers. When she remonstrates, the director replies that what matters is whether they make a film, not what the film is about. Waking, she names the dream as being about total sterility, the sterility of the artist who no longer feels she can write truthfully.

The single entry in the red notebook shows through the excess of its story's protagonist that Anna is at last letting go of her emotional allegiance to communism.

Harry Matthews has prepared for the day when he would be summoned to the Kremlin to give his views on how the Russian Communist Party had gone wrong. Invited to join a tour to the Soviet Union, he believes till the last evening that this is the call he has awaited all his life. Disillusioned at last, he lectures from a panoply of books and notes to the only person left to listen to him when, forgetting she is only an exhausted tour guide, he addresses "History itself" (454). His experience, which reflects to an exaggerated degree the feelings of many communists who joined the party in the 30s, reveals in a parodic form the strength of the hope that has maintained Anna's illusions and the cynicism with which she now regards them.

The yellow notebook has its version of newspaper clippings, notes of ideas for short stories. It ends with a parody about American working-class youths called "The Romantic Tough School of Writing" (462), which is clearly a parody based on Saul Green.

The blue notebook begins to connect even more closely with the other notebooks, recording for example the incidents to which the story ideas in the yellow notebook are cross-referenced. The ideas come to Anna when, with Janet gone to boarding school, she rents a room to Saul Green. From this point on all the concerns engaging Anna's attention are treated within the dialogue she establishes with Saul. This breakdown of the compartmentalization giving some kind of order to Anna's life signals a breakdown in Anna herself. She reflects on the way in which so many people try to control emotion "in a world as terrible as this" (466). She understands that her desire not to feel is general: "People know they are in a society dead or dying. They are refusing emotion because at the end of every emotion are property, money, power" (466–67). She tries to regain her childhood ability to visualize at once the whole world and a single leaf or a drop of water, thus attaining "simultaneous knowledge of vastness and of smallness" (469—another articulation of the cosmic view that Lessing later pursues in *Canopus in Argos*.

Saul resurrects in Anna not only her writer's imagination but also a range of emotions to which she has been dead for years. She falls hopelessly in love with Saul "so that . . . the warmth of his shoulder against my palm is all the joy there is in life" (479); conversely, she begins to have nightmares of being both the "old dwarfed malicious man" (481) and the old malicious woman, and of Saul as an embodiment of the same malicious principle. She is invaded by alien emotions, for example a "terrible, spiteful jealousy" (482) of Saul's other women. She and Saul argue about everything from the state of the world to her class origins and his childish machismo.

At last she understands that she has entered his madness and can no longer separate herself from him, but she also understands that it is a temporary state because she will have to be sane when Janet returns. By then Anna will have completed the pattern she must work through. She tries to summon the image of Tom Mathlong to balance Saul's influence but instead becomes inhabited by the terror-filled paranoia of Charlie Themba, who imagines that his wife and his Congressional colleagues are trying to poison him with tainted crocodile meat. Suddenly returning to sanity, she falls asleep and dreams that she is "the malicious male-female dwarf figure, the principle of joy-in-destruction; and Saul was my counter-part, male-female, my brother and my sister" (508). She is approaching the point where she will be able to experience the positive aspect of disintegration.

Once more the blue notebook provides a summation. For the first time Anna admits that she has been suffering from a writer's block. Now that she no longer needs to compartmentalize, she admits to the reason for keeping four notebooks. Realizing the way to integration lies through breakdown rather than false order, she intends from now on to put "all of [her]self in one book" (519). This decision, which is as unmeditated as the one to keep four notebooks, marks her recognition that the way to wholeness is through a healing madness.

### "The Golden Notebook"

Although Anna refers to her fusion with Saul as a sickness, the experience leads to therapeutic insights. Her dreams once more reveal her condition: she is

# THE GOLDEN NOTEBOOK

drowning in a few inches of water at the bottom of a tiger's cage, while the tiger itself is draped over the top. Gathering all her will, she flies out, only to realize that the tiger, which she names as Saul, is being hunted by men who intend to return him to the cage. Anna mourns because she wants Saul running free through the world. Half awake, she begins to plan a play featuring Anna, Saul, and the tiger but, accusing herself of always making up stories about life, resolves to put the idea aside. This episode is another example of Lessing's intertextuality: in fact, Lessing did write *Play with a Tiger*, a play which was published in the same year as *The Golden Notebook*.

Anna understands that she still needs to work on retrieving her past. Again she dreams that she is watching a movie, controlled by a mad projectionist, who also turns out to be Saul. As the scenes roll by, she learns that she has not, for instance, truly understood June Boothby, nor consciously noticed significant details such as Willi's hurt look when she flirted with Paul Brockenhurst or Mr. Lattimer's repeated stroking of the red-haired dog that so much resembled his faithless wife; nor had she completely imagined Paul Tanner's homecoming early in the morning, "brisk and efficient with guilt" (543). As Saul's acting as dream projectionist suggests, his and Anna's *folie à deux* has forged a permanent link between them. Lovers, but brother and sister in their psyches and consciences, twins in their psychotic breakdown, they help each other reorder their lives. Both have suffered from a writer's block; each gives the other the first sentence for a new novel. Saul's is the first sentence of "Free Women" and, of course, *The Golden Notebook.* In the new golden notebook Saul has demanded and she has until now refused to give, Anna writes her sentence: "On a dry hillside in Algeria, a soldier watched the moonlight glinting on his rifle" (549). The notebook concludes with a synopsis of this novel, a story of conscience set in the Algerian war of liberation from France, which is saturated with the existentialism—the legacy of the French experience in World War Two—popular in the 50s. This story in which both French prisoner and Algerian guard are shot is of course appropriate to a man who has believed he would be dead by the age of thirty, but it is also appropriate to Anna, who has for many years been involved with anticolonial issues.

The golden notebook gives a streamlined version of Anna's life—her past, her ideals, her dreams, her disintegration into madness, her reintegration into a new self, her hope for the future, the dissolution of her writer's block; it "button[s] up" (535) her commitment to communism and her romantic love with Michael and Saul. She has shed some worn-out responses, refusing, for example, to play victim to Saul's cannibal, a role she has investigated through Ella of the yellow notebook. Understanding that her memory of Mashopi was formed by who she was at the time, she no longer reproaches herself for the "lying nostalgia" of *The Frontiers of War;* instead, even though she now recognizes that absolute objectivity is impossible, she believes it would be useful to re-remember by working on her past in order to establish a world view valid for herself. With reintegration comes the end of Anna's writer's block, the proof of which is "Free Women," and perhaps *The Golden Notebook* as well.

### "Free Women" 5

This segment wraps up the framing novel. Anna, more conventional here than in the life described in her notebooks, demonstrates what her experiences have taught her. Although Molly, who remarries, urges her to begin writing again, Anna opts instead for a life of service; admiring the "small endurance that is bigger than anything" (544), she plans to become what Molly calls "a matrimonial welfare worker" (568), join the Labour Party, and teach a night class for delinquent children twice a week—a fictional analogue of the kind of endurance Anna has learned to admire during her journey through madness. "Free Women" demonstrates the essence of boulder-pushing, which is to take on simple, ordinary tasks, as Martha Quest does in *The Four-Gated City*.

"Free Women" is more conventional both in content and form than *The Golden Notebook*, from whose notebooks it is shaped. In it Anna presents her life as more ordinary than it appears in the notebooks; it follows a traditional chronological plan and a tighter pattern of cause and effect. Further, the compression and shaping of experience required by the conventional novel leads to a heightening of the ordinary, which results in more melodramatic events. Tommy, a comparatively minor figure in the notebooks, is heightened in just this way into a double of Anna: his suicide attempt and subsequent blindness are a symbolic projection of Anna's situation that conflates the ideas of destruction and madness, making them more extreme and thus more readily comprehensible. Nonetheless this comprehension depends ultimately on a set of conventions about the nature of madness and its connection with suicide, conventions *The Golden Notebook*'s investigation of madness contradicts. Thus it is not only omission and concentration that make the conventional novel false but also the act of ordering the chaos of experience according to worn perceptions and outgrown precepts. In the dialogue between "Free Women" and the notebooks Lessing makes a statement not only about this conventional novel but about the conventional novel in general. *The Golden Notebook* is her most complete statement about the nature of art and its relation to experience.

## *THE GOLDEN NOTEBOOK*

# *Notes*

1. R. D. Laing, *The Divided Self* (London: Pelican, 1971) 42.

2. Betsy Draine, *Substance under Pressure: Artistic Coherence and Evolving Forms in the Novels of Doris Lessing* (Madison: University of Wisconsin Press, 1983) 69.

3. Lessing, "On *The Golden Notebook,* " *A Small Personal Voice,* ed. Paul Schlueter (New York: Knopf, 1974) 32–33. This essay has appeared as the introduction to editions of *The Golden Notebook* since 1972. (Page references given in parentheses refer to *A Small Personal Voice.*)

4. Claire Sprague, *Rereading Doris Lessing* (Chapel Hill: University of North Carolina Press, 1987) 81.

5. Sprague 65–84.

6. Joseph Hynes, "The Construction of *The Golden Notebook,*" *Iowa Review* 4 (1973): 101.

7. For arguments that Anna is the writer of the entire *Golden Notebook,* see Draine 87, 197–98.

8. Hynes 103.

9. Lessing, *The Golden Notebook* (New York: Simon and Schuster, 1962) 9; subsequent references are noted in parentheses.

10. Draine 81.

11. For a full discussion of the relationship between Lessing's and Laing's views see Marion Vlastos, "Doris Lessing and R. D. Laing: Psychopolitics and Prophecy," *Critical Essays on Doris Lessing,* ed. Claire Sprague and Virginia Tiger (Boston: Hall, 1986) 126–41.

# CHAPTER FIVE

# *Briefing for a Descent into Hell* (1971); *The Summer before the Dark* (1973); *The Memoirs of a Survivor* (1974)

In these three novels written between *Children of Violence* (1952–69) and *Canopus in Argos* (1979–83), Lessing is less interested in the particularities of individuals, in the ways in which individuals are different, more in the ways they are the same; all three are concerned with the nature of inner space, into the regions of which, as Martha Quest's experience demonstrates, the further one goes, the more one discovers they are inhabited by all humanity. She continues, especially in *Summer* and *Memoirs,* her interest in roles, especially in women's roles as they change throughout the life cycle. She further reminds her readers of humanity's appropriate place in nature by her continuing use of animal imagery which, appearing in dreams and hallucinations, suggests the unconscious sense of kinship with other life forms.

In these novels Lessing further investigates the implications of interconnectedness between the inner and the outer first developed at length in *The Golden Notebook* and *The Four-Gated City*. However, unlike the inner journeys of the earlier works that result in reconciliation with the outer, in these novels the exploration of inner space involves in varying degrees a rejection of the outer world, which in its collective falsity has made these protagonists lose sight of their transcendental selves—the true selves that must abandon the collective in order to align themselves with the greater whole. All of them are engaged in the Sufi task of transcending humanity's ordinary limitations in the interests of evolutionary development, Lessing's view of which is teleological rather than open-ended, having as its goal the rediscovery of the root of one's being, the reintegration with the whole.

### *Briefing for a Descent into Hell* (1971)

The structure of this novel in many ways resembles that of *The Golden Notebook*. Assorted narratives told through multiple documents are framed and interspersed by the story of Charles Watkins's stay in a psychiatric hospital, much in the way that "Free Women" frames and intersperses Anna Wulf's notebooks. Although these assorted narratives have some correspondences, like Anna's notebooks they do not quite match.

Nonetheless, as Charles's story unfolds subtle differences begin to appear between his kind of madness and Anna's—indeed, between his and that of any

Lessing character to this point. For Anna and Martha madness is a respite from the world, a way of healing divisions for a return to ordinary life. Lynda Coldridge's and Mary Turner's kinds of madness are a more permanent way of dealing with self-division, both women taking refuge from a collective that has maimed them by insisting they adopt traditional feminine roles they would have preferred to decline. Although to some extent Charles also seems to be escaping from the demands of family life and his job as professor of philology at Cambridge University, to which the psychiatric establishment wishes to return him, his madness seems less of a retreat than a quest; indeed one of the major images of his sleeping life—during which he insists he is actually most awake—is a circular voyage of discovery.

Charles's madness is both less personal and less connected with the outer world than Anna's; it is more archetypal, less historical. The important Sufi image of the Ocean of Infinite Possibility,[1] which may be both within and without, informs all his mental activity (neither *consciousness* nor *unconsciousness* is the correct word here, since what are generally thought of as unconscious processes are precisely what he is conscious of). He specifically claims kinship with sailors from myth and legend such as Odysseus, Sinbad, Jonah, and Jason. He proclaims this state as the human condition: "We are all sailors."[2] Other traditional images appearing in the narrative of his inner journey are the parodic versions of Greek gods and the ruined city built on the plan of a Jungian mandala.

Although it might be possible to make a case for *Briefing* as an exploration of a Laingian madness preparing the patient for a return to ordinary life, there are two substantive reasons against this reading. Such a madness is a self-limiting disease, whereas Charles, overlooking the well-known tendency of electroshock treatments to destroy inordinate numbers of brain cells rather than to enhance mental life, submits to shock therapy in the belief that it might make him remember important parts of his psychic life. Of course, as he is warned by his fellow patient Violent Stokes, it has no such effect; he appears to remember instead what the psychiatrists and his family want him to remember.

The second reason is even more telling. Lessing's title, *Briefing for a Descent into Hell*, allies Charles with the Descent Team from the Olympian Conference, the transcription of which appears as part of his meditation while in the hospital. Like the Canopean Johor, who reincarnates as George Sherban in *Shikasta*, he is apparently a divinity reborn as Charles Watkins already brainprinted to deliver the message of Cosmic Harmony invisible to humanity, whose senses are insufficiently developed to perceive its myriad manifestations, many of them incongruous to collective ways of thinking.

This argument, however, does not in itself explain the extraordinary deployment of multiple narratives in the novel. There is evidence to suggest that, like *The*

*Golden Notebook,* the shape of *Briefing* parallels its meaning.

In *Briefing* Draine charts plural narrative levels, none of which is subordinated to any other. The first begins with the hospital admission sheet naming Charles Watkins, amnesia patient, shifting to his (at this point) presumably psychotic ramblings about sea voyages, then to the fantastic but realistically described explorations of the city where the rat-dogs and apes battle and the narrator (presumably Charles) tries to keep the mandala square clean for the landing of the harmony-bringing Crystal. The narrative switches to the fable of the giant white bird, then back to the hospital, then into the Crystal for "mystical meditation"—part of which is an "offensively silly story of the [classical] jokester gods, played in the tone of farce."[3] There follow a tale of birth and infancy, a return to the hospital, and a series of letters explaining Watkins's life before he was found wandering on the Thames Embankment. Then comes a new tale of Watkins as a Yugoslav partisan, followed by a scene at the hospital where Watkins abandons his anticollective alliance with Violet Stokes in order to undergo shock therapy. Draine concludes that Lessing switches the narrative levels in this way in order to undermine the primacy of any one meaning—as Charles himself says, "It isn't either or at all, it's and, and, and, and, and" (165). She suggests that *Briefing* is modeled on the Sufi teaching story which, having many different levels of significance rather than a singular meaning, was designed "to change the spiritual disciple's mode of perception"; meaning comes from "the interconnections of situations, characters, and action among the several versions of [Charles Watkins's] story."[4] Thus the elaborate interconnections between disparate narratives, a simple example of which is the correspondence and contradiction between Constance Mayne of a letter sequence and the Yugoslav partisan Konstantina, point to the hidden harmony which humanity has lost sight of in the false selves determined by the collective. On one point *Briefing* is quite clear: confronted by a different consciousness, the collective will use both psychological and physical force to curb aberrant behavior.

*Briefing* contains the most complete statement to date of Lessing's gradually evolved idea of the cosmic whole. The Olympic Conference specifies the task of the permanent staff on Earth: to help humanity evolve "into an understanding of their individual selves as merely parts of a whole, first of all humanity, their own species [and then to achieve] a conscious knowledge of humanity as part of Nature; plants, animals, birds, insects, reptiles, all these together making a small chord in the Cosmic Harmony" (141). The nature of this cosmic whole is ultimately determined by the forces emanating from the sun and its planets:

Lines and currents of force and empathy and antago-
nism danced in a web that was the system of planets
around the sun, so much a part of the sun that its glow
of substance, lying all about it in space, held the planets
as intimately as if these planets were merely crystalliza-
tions or hardening of its vaporous stuff, moments of
density in the solar wind. And this web was an iron, a
frightful necessity. (116)

Catastrophes like war or overpopulation are caused by
a shift in planetary balance; the comet that altered the
rotational axis of the earth pushed humanity off-center
and, in a version of the Fall reminiscent of the medieval
world view, detached humankind from its proper place
in the cosmic harmony, making it subject to mutability
and a misplaced valuation of individualism.

   Although it is clear that this analysis of the whole
is at least in part metaphorical, it is also clear that the
element of transcendence present in Martha Quest's visionary experience on the veld has reappeared in
Lessing's work in a new formulation. Nonetheless it is
equally clear that *Briefing* is not intended to describe the
organization of the universe but to defamiliarize the
world so that readers will look at it with new eyes and
open minds. This novel opens up a new avenue of hypothetical exploration for Lessing, one that she fully
exploits in *Canopus in Argos*. A caption on the frontis-
piece reads "Category: Inner Space Fiction—For there
is never anywhere to go but in." Once more, however,

it appears that the inner and the outer are the same, for after the next two novels she started writing undisguised space fiction without the mediation of the psychiatric hospital.

### *The Summer before the Dark* (1973)

Although it reworks some aspects of Charles Watkins's experience from a woman's perspective, this novel is similar to *Briefing* in a number of significant ways. Kate Brown's experience parallels Watkins's: she too undergoes a period of mental illness during which her dreams, featuring the regenerative power of the transcendental as represented by the sea, put her in touch with her true self; after a circular journey during which she engaged in extensive meditation on the gap between her outer and inner lives, she also returns to the family home. She too belongs to the professional middle classes, earning this status by virtue of her marriage to a successful neurologist—so successful that his international reputation brings him invitations to do professional work in the United States every summer.

Lessing's acute grip on the British class system is very evident in this novel. The Browns, with four well-educated children, live in Blackheath where, apart from London's West End, the most expensive housing in the United Kingdom is located. Kate, who at the time when she was about to enter the university with a major in

Romance languages married Michael Brown instead, has spent twenty-five years being a wife and mother; now, when it becomes clear that all other family members will be away for the summer, she realizes that the role on which she has based her sense of self has disappeared. Because the house, which represents her life, will be rented out, she agrees to take a temporary job as a simultaneous translator for Global Foods. This job gives her the information to put her situation in worldwide perspective when she attends a conference in Turkey. The extraordinary abundance of commodities like food and clothing that her privileged status allows her to take for granted becomes even more obvious when she travels through Spain with her young lover and later when, taking a room in a basement flat in London, she comes face to face with a social stratum she has never interacted with before.

Kate's social circumstances need to be stressed because, starting with a review by Erica Jong in *The New York Review of Books*, several critics have wanted to read Kate Brown as an Everywoman, a typical British housewife. Rather, Lessing stresses her untypicality—the luxury of her home, her ability to translate between Portuguese, French, and Italian as she hears a speaker's words, her marriage to an internationally known physician bespeak very privileged circumstances indeed. In this regard she is like Susan Rawlings of "To Room Nineteen" who, however, when family life fails her, cannot find a way to her real self except by turning on the gas in a rented room until she "drift[s] off into the dark river." For both these women, no matter how privileged their lives, the role of wife and mother has been inimical to their transcendental selves which, neglected, have withered away.

For Lessing such neglect is not a particularly female fate: in addition to Charles Watkins, the protagonist of "The Temptation of Jack Orkney" suffers such a crisis in middle age. The most rational of socialists, whose life has been structured around his political commitments, at his father's death he undergoes a kind of breakdown, becoming vulnerable to his dreams, the existence of which he has never before acknowledged. Now feeling "like a threatened building" he begins to consider transcendental questions at the approach of old age: "he could feel his face falling into the lines and folds of his father's face." He recovers from his breakdown when he integrates his dreaming with his daytime life.

Kate Brown's recognition of a transcendental self also comes through dream and breakdown. She has a serial dream in which she must carry a scarred and battered seal northward to the sea, so turning to her own account the nurturance that her family has spurned. Thus her dreams parallel the one of Mrs. Quest's in which she was both the mother and the baby being nurtured. Fabular and archetypal in contrast to the specifying detail of Kate's daytime life, these dreams are exacerbated by physical illness into breakdown, from which Kate recovers to find herself haggard from loss of weight and branded by a wide band of grey bisecting her dark red hair. Renting a room from Maureen, a young woman from a class if anything higher than her own, she works out on a conscious level some of her ambivalence about her children; Maureen, in return, articulates her hostility to the middle-aged matron, so feared by Martha Quest. *Summer* shows that middle-aged matron in a sympathetic light: Kate Brown is another version of May Quest, who dies still trying to cling to the role of the powerful matron. Like Martha, who works through the role of mother with Coldridge surrogates, Kate unravels her difficulty with her daughter Eileen through the similarly named Maureen; unlike May Quest, she breaks out of her role into the freedom of old age.

Kate acknowledges this development by refusing to dye her hair again or to make any other concession to her family's conception of how she should look. Much of her meditation on constricting roles for women has taken the form of a concern with looks, specifically with hair and clothes. Maureen has similar preoccupations, putting on various outfits as though trying out various roles, in one especially agitated state even cutting off her long blonde hair and plaiting it into a "harvest doll" (the traditional function of which is to be buried in a furrow to ensure abundant crops the following year). Since Kate returns to her house in Blackheath, the greying of her hair seems to some readers too small a change in her outer life for the momentous upheaval in the inner.[5] However, in spite of the particularity of Kate's historical circumstances which might lead one to expect an outcome like Anna's or Martha's, in *Summer* breakdown is not, as in *The Golden Notebook* or *The Four-Gated City*, a self-healing illness that returns the sufferer to ordinary life. Instead, as in *Briefing* or "Jack Orkney," the discovery of the spiritual dimension makes a profound change in the inner life. In her last serial dream Kate succeeds in returning her seal to the northern sea where it joins a herd "swerving and diving, playing."[6] She cannot recognize her seal; it has become anonymous, part of a whole—a concept that becomes even more important in *Canopus*. As Draine points out, this return is accompanied by an image of hope and rebirth:[7] "a large, light, buoyant, tumultuous sun that seemed to sing."[8] Kate has returned her seal to the inner-space sea of her unconscious, on which, rather than on temporary roles, the identity of the true self rests. Her family's rejection has forced her to resurrect the self that has been withering since girlhood, enabling her to transcend the collective as old age approaches.

## The Memoirs of a Survivor (1974)

This novel appears to be set in a future similar to the one described in the appendix to *The Four-Gated City*. Here, however, the catastrophe is not caused by a nuclear accident but by the gradual collapse of all social systems. As Marx predicted, capitalism breaks down from internal pressure;[9] democratic socialism, which temporarily arises in some informal groups, is even more ephemeral. London—unnamed but identifiable by the Fleet River and the Underground—gradually regresses through previous stages of civilization. First the electricity and gas are cut off; people start growing vegetables, keeping hens, cows, and drayhorses; barter replaces buying and selling. Then nomadic life reappears: groups of people pass through from areas even more afflicted, their goods tied on wagons and handcarts; local inhabitants gather on the sidewalks preparing to take off north where, it is rumored, food supplies are still available; gangs of increasingly younger children appear, supporting themselves mainly by theft. Eventually a tribe of cannibals, some as young as four or five years old, emerge from the Underground.

The narrator, a self-conscious reporter setting down what she remembers after these events have run their course, is unnamed, though as the novel progresses who she is becomes clear. When the social breakdown accelerates beyond a general distrust of authority, the Survivor becomes aware of what Orkney calls "another country, lying just behind his daytime one." In *Memoirs*, where the predominant image system, as in *Summer*, is based on houses and rooms, this other country lies "behind the wall."[10] Whereas Jack and Kate need to dream to enter this country, the Survivor goes through the wall in her waking state and discovers there a set of rooms she recognizes as containing something she has "been waiting for . . . all [her] life" (13). Her repeated visits play a part in the narrative structure similar to that of Kate's serial dream in *Summer*.

The full significance of her experience takes some time to sink in because, unlike Kate, who immediately recognizes the seal's relation to herself, the Survivor does not connect the rooms beyond the wall with other events in her life. Immediately after Emily Mary Cartwright's first visit, a stranger announces that the thirteen-year-old will from now on be the Survivor's responsibility. Reflecting that this incident is no more extraordinary than others currently taking place, the Survivor accepts Emily with a marked degree of sympathy and identification, even taking in Emily's strange pet, the cat-dog Hugo. When Emily starts visiting with the migrating gangs of young people on the pavement, the Survivor begins to understand that the events outside, the relationship between her and Emily, and what she sees beyond the wall may all be connected. The marvelous high-ceilinged, whitewashed rooms are full of vandalized furniture, which the Survivor cleans and repairs. She begins to feel presences in these empty rooms, presences that bring the atmosphere of the "personal" (41; Lessing's quotation marks), defined as a kind of prison, as opposed to the impersonal tasks "like the rehabilitation of walls or furniture, cleaning, putting order into chaos [which imply] the possibility of alternative action" (41).

This distinction between the "personal" and the impersonal is important in Lessing's thought. The "personal" comprises familial and all other roles generally considered personal relations. These roles divert one from rediscovering one's true self, which identity depends on the transcendental. The family appearing behind the wall is especially destructive. Dated by the infant's Edwardian layette, it consists of a baby boy, a young girl, and a soldier father and jolly, courageous mother, neither of whom, because of their own upbringing, can be held responsible for the damage they do their children. In short, the nightmare repetition is again in evidence. The Survivor eventually recognizes the little girl as the Emily entrusted to her care; readers, keeping in mind that Lessing has called this novel "an attempt at autobiography," will recognize the Tayler family, which is also the prototype for the Quests. Emily Mary is named after Lessing's mother, Emily Maude. Lessing takes pains to draw attention to discrepant details hinting at an intertextual identification, pointing out the fact that the scene the Survivor watches cannot come from her protégée Emily's own childhood: "such [a] childhood . . . these days . . . was obsolete" (45). The Survivor feels her work beyond the wall, for which furniture repair is clearly a metaphor, as a liberation because of its implied possibilities; it constitutes her real task, just as carrying her seal toward the sea is Kate's.

## *MEMOIRS OF A SURVIVOR*

Under the pressure of the disintegrating infrastructure Emily grows up quickly, living in telescoped fashion through all Martha Quest's roles, many of which she too tries out through changes of clothing. She becomes the woman of Gerald, the leader of a gang who with her help (here she is as efficient as the Martha of *Ripple*) organizes a commune, complete with kitchen garden and rosters for task rotation. Meanwhile Hugo, who wants to be Emily's "only friend and love" (52), watches over her with dejected devotion. Just as the cannibal children are less than human, so is Hugo more than what is generally considered animal. This "botch of a creature" (81) is Lessing's main device in *Memoirs* to remind readers of their relationship with animals and thus of humanity's place in nature.

The final accommodation between the inner and outer life takes place within a transcendent nature reminiscent of Martha Quest's visionary experience on the veld. Social breakdown intensifies as the cannibal children take over. Gerald has been unable to mold them into a community but cannot bear to abandon hope in them because of their tender age. Behind the wall the rooms have become insubstantial, giving way to primeval forest—much as the Tayler house on the veld was in danger of returning to the bush—where the Survivor feels "the one Presence . . . [of] the Whole" (99)—the impersonal at its most essential that brings release both from the "personal" and from the crumbling social fabric on which the roles of the "personal" depend. The last scene integrates the Emilys from both sides of the wall when, the walls dissolving, Emily, Hugo, Gerald, and the cannibal children all follow the One "out of this collapsed little world into another order of world altogether" (213).

Here it becomes clear that the Emily behind the wall is not only the Survivor's protégée but also the Survivor herself: the description of the final exodus makes no mention of the Survivor passing through the wall as a separate entity, but clearly she, the only person who has been on the other side until this point, has not been left behind. Following the structure of Kate Brown's and Mrs. Quest's dreams of self-parenting, the Survivor, working on both her own and her mother's past, has recuperated her transcendence by freeing her childhood self from an unconscious prison.

## Notes

1. Martin Lings, *What is Sufism?* (Berkeley: University of California Press, 1977) 11–15.

2. Lessing, *Briefing for a Descent into Hell* (New York: Knopf, 1975) 8; subsequent references are noted in parentheses.

3. Betsy Draine, *Substance under Pressure: Artistic Coherence and Evolving Forms in the Novels of Doris Lessing* (Madison: University of Wisconsin Press, 1983) 91.

4. Draine 92.

5. Mona Knapp, *Doris Lessing* (New York: Ungar, 1984) 118.

## THE MEMOIRS OF A SURVIVOR

6. Lessing, *The Summer before the Dark* (New York: Knopf, 1973) 266.

7. Draine 128.

8. Lessing *Summer* 267.

9. Knapp 122.

10. Lessing, *The Memoirs of a Survivor* (New York: Knopf, 1975) 7; subsequent references are noted in parentheses.

# CHAPTER SIX

# *Canopus in Argos: Archives*

The connections between concepts related in Lessing's work begin to become clearer in the *Canopus in Argos* series. Particularly troublesome have been those between nature, civilization, history, and necessity, which last is especially problematic in *Canopus*. It has always been an important idea for Lessing, but its contours have become apparent only gradually as the connections between the elements it comprises have been exposed.

Early in *Children of Violence necessity* appears in the description of Martha Quest's first visionary experience on the veld, for example, and in the contexts of biology and history in *A Proper Marriage*. The word accumulates a degree of resonance from these contexts. In *Canopus* necessity appears to be a function of Cosmic Harmony; however, these two related values are difficult both to grasp and to empathize with because, unlike civilization and nature, which are concrete in the city and the veld, they are not represented by images. The nearest attempt at such an encoding appears in *Briefing*, where,

## CANOPUS IN ARGOS

however, the symbol is too allegorical to function as dynamic image. Thus both concepts remain rhetorical.

In positing that "we are all creatures of the stars and their forces,"[1] Lessing seems to suggest that necessity is a cosmic extension of nature. But *necessity*, as its appearance in other contexts indicates, also includes the idea of human history; therefore, as the executive arm of Cosmic Harmony, the transcendent whole to which both planets and individuals are subject, necessity appears to be a view, extended into space, of the city on the veld, which holds both nature and civilization in a dynamic whole. Thus Canopean necessity deconstructs the opposition between nature and history, a reconciliation adumbrated in *Briefing*, where both natural disasters and man-made catastrophes are explained as a consequence of planetary realignment. Although this explanation seems to imply a deterministic universe, individuals can in fact make a choice, as the case of Ambien II—a member of a species that, though not human, possesses many human characteristics—abundantly demonstrates, either to work against the Cosmic Harmony or to go with the flow of the transcendental Ocean.

### Re: Colonised Planet 5, Shikasta (1979)

This novel reworks the situation of *The Four-Gated City* from a larger cosmic view, extending the frame of reference in both space and time. Lessing hypothesizes the existence of other sentient beings in the universe, whose views on the human present and past give a defamiliarized version of history. The main action begins during the Last Days, toward the end of the Century of Destruction (the twentieth century), when a nuclear catastrophe wipes out civilization, leaving only one percent of the population alive on a polluted planet. Into this situation Johor, a Canopean who for centuries has been involved in Shikastan affairs, is incarnated as George Sherban. The Canopean interest in Shikasta is that of the benevolent imperialist who promotes the welfare of the colonized—a posture unnervingly reminiscent of British attitudes toward subject races in Lessing's African writings.

*Shikasta* rewrites the Old Testament, Darwinian theory, and history, accommodating them to each other by the related ploys of focusing on the Fall rather than on the Creation, and subordinating evolution to the necessity to which planets themselves are subordinate. In this view of evolution Lessing deftly highlights the one similarity between Marx and Jung, making more understandable her unlikely ideological switch from the one to the other. Both theories are explicitly teleological. Marx sees history as a social evolution toward the already known end of the workers' state; Jung understands individuation as the progression toward the individual self already determined by one's nature. In *Shikasta*, Lessing propounds the idea of human evolution (indeed of all species, whether earthly or alien) as the consummation of a plan designed by superior imperialists in the service of necessity. This planned evolution is both an expression of the urge to transcendence that appears throughout her work and a way to sidestep the nightmare of Freudian repetition.

Appropriately for a text entertaining cosmic and transcendental questions, *Shikasta* deals with the problem underlying all religions: If God is both all good and all powerful, how did evil enter the world? The aliens in charge of human destiny seem to be other species rather than divine beings, although there is a suggestive numinosity about Johor especially evident in his ability to incarnate as a Shikastan. Both the great empires colonizing earth (defamiliarized as prelapsarian Rohanda and postlapsarian Shikasta) are subject to stellar influences, a shift in which results in the failure of the Lock, a connection between Canopus and Rohanda designed to feed the colonized species with the crucial "substance-of-we-feeling" (SOWF). The criminal Puttioran planet Shammat manages to tap into this source of energy, subverting Rohandans into willful individualism—the Degenerative Disease—rather than the happy acceptance of necessity, which seems to be the highest virtue of Lessing's new world. Thus Lessing defamiliarizes Satan, at the same time, because Rohandans did not fall as a consequence of exercising the privilege of choice, doing away with the Christian concept of free will, though they are free to work toward an understanding of necessity. Further, because the planetary alignments are responsible for the dwindling supply of SOWF (apparently Lessing's version of Christian grace), the universe of *Canopus* seems remarkably close to the one Voltaire satirized in *Candide* as the best of all possible worlds. This universe, however, is not quite as deterministic as the one inhabited by Mary Turner: there is some suggestion that individuals bear responsibility—if not for their state, at least for transcending it. Although the fate of the species is in the hands of superior beings, individuals may escape from Shikasta by their own efforts rather than by rescue at the hands of an outside agency. This route seems to be a kind of Jungian individuation or an exercise in Sufi mysticism, much like the "work" Martha Quest does under Lynda Coldridge's tutelage in *The Four-Gated City*. When Johor is waiting at the gates of Zone Six to be born as a Shikastan, he sees crowds of Shikastan souls turning away from the miseries of the declining planet, imploring superior beings to release them, just as in *Briefing* Charles Watkins yearns to be taken off in the Crystal. Seeing Ben, a friend he made on a previous visit, Johor reminds him " 'to try again, there is no other way,' . . . [to] crystallize into a substance that could survive and withstand" (9).

Once more Lessing uses the technique of multiple documents introduced in the appendix to *The Four-Gated City* and deployed with such effect in *The Golden Notebook* and *Briefing*. Some of these documents come from the Canopean archives, such as Johor's reports to his superiors, supplemented by excerpts from Canopean histories and guidebooks; others are secret official letters about Rohanda/Shikasta sent between Canopus, colonizer of Rohanda's northern hemisphere, and Sirius, colonizer of the southern. Rachel Sherban's journal centers on Johor in his incarnation as her brother George Sherban. In addition there are personal letters from varied sources such as the state official Chen Liu, Sharma Patel, and Lynda Coldridge from *The Four-Gated City*. These three different kinds of documents represent three familiar dialogic positions in Lessing's fiction. Rachel Sherban's personal journal provides the individual view, Chen Liu's political letters the collective, and the Canopean documents that of the whole, the Cosmic Harmony.

The most vivid image of harmony in *Shikasta* takes a familiar form. The Mathematical Cities, whose architecture maintains cosmic unity through "the deep harmonies of the stones" (31) parallels Martha Quest's city in the veld no matter what their geometric shape (as Knapp has trenchantly observed, only the pentagon seems to be missing[2]). All creatures are subject to this harmony, not only the natives and the giants who have been sent to Rohanda to help with the forced growth phase of the natives, but all the animals as well. Through the stones of these cities the Canopean vibrations maintain the Lock with Rohanda, which Johor visualizes as "the silvery cord of our love" (67), a fitting image, even if it suggests a maternal posture rather than the paternalism favored by Canopus toward inferior species.

The issue of parenting that figures so large in *The Four-Gated City* is of utmost importance in *Shikasta*. As in the appendix to the former novel, hope for the future lies explicitly with the children, and it is to them that the influence of Canopus is directed. A story central to the meaning of the book is a defamiliarized version of the nativity in which the object of celebration is all children rather than the Christ Child alone: "every child has the capacity to be everything. A child [is] a miracle, a wonder!" (167).

The importance of an education to develop individual talents rather than to indoctrinate with the values of the collective is stressed in the way the Sherbans bring up their remarkable son. He learns what he needs to know to complete his mission from teachers who appear, uninvited, in his life. Everywhere in this ruined world the young assume responsibility, taking care of those still younger, as Rachel Sherban looks after the orphans Leila and Kassim, and Benjamin Sherban organizes children's refugee camps. Youth armies "throw up leaders not those designated by authority" (235), on whom Canopus concentrates "its plans of rescue and reform" (236).

*Shikasta* is perhaps more optimistic for the future of the human race than was *The Four-Gated City*. Johor's special mission, for which he has been preparing since his birth as a human, teaches the young a vital lesson for the survival of the species that their elders have never learned. He engineers the bringing to trial of the white races, who are accused of causing the destruction, corruption, and pollution of the planet. After all the crimes committed by the dominant white races have been exposed, the assembled youth come to understand that they have no monopoly on oppression; indeed, the Marxist Chinese, who condemn them the most fiercely, have adopted their worst characteristics. In short, the youth are "in for a seminar on man's inhumanity to man" (338). The trial dissolves, and the "planned wiping out of the remaining European population" (340) simply fades away. The ostensible Canopean interest in preventing the massacre is "of course the preservation of adequate representative genetic material" (347).

The end of *Shikasta* echoes the conclusion of *The Four-Gated City*. Lest the parallel be overlooked, Lessing includes amongst the last documents a letter from Lynda Coldridge to Benjamin Sherban. Lynda foretells the "Third and Final Phase" of the "Twentieth Century War" (355), which is survived by Suzannah, who, pregnant with George Sherban's posthumous child, directs a children's camp in the Andes. The novel ends with Kassim's helping to build "a star city, five points" (363)—a version of the city that Mark could only dream of—in a landscape similar to Martha Quest's veld: "It is high up here, very high, with marvellous tall sky over us, a pale clear crystalline blue, and the great birds circling in it" (363). With the help of Canopus, the young will evolve into superior beings, just as did the children at the end of *The Four-Gated City*, especially in view of the reduced population, whom "the substance-of-we-feeling [is] now enough to sustain, and keep . . . sweet, and whole, and healthy" (93). As Kassim puts it, "There are more and more George-people all the time" (360).

### The Marriages Between Zones Three, Four and Five (1980)

Unlike the writerly text of *Shikasta* with its manifold documents from which the reader must infer the narrative line, *Marriages* is a readerly text with a double-functioned narrator. Lusick, a Chronicler of Zone Three, explains events to his peers but also mediates for Lessing's readers. His remarks on the differences between actual events and their traditional portrayal also constitute part of Lessing's ongoing dialogue about the responsibility of the artist. Lusick must speak both to his community and for it, expressing what its members cannot articulate for themselves and interpreting events to them in the light of their cultural values. At the same time he is the leader, not the follower: the writer's task is to provide spiritual insight rather than to give voice to public opinion.

The precise locale of *Marriages* in the Canopean cosmography is unclear. Canopus is never mentioned by name; the superior beings in control are called simply the Providers—a benevolent name, suggestive of Providence, for those who issue orders without regard for the feelings of the ordered. The point of connection with Canopus lies in names of the realms whose interrelationships are the subject of the novel. When Johor, as detailed in *Shikasta*, incarnates as a Shikastan, he enters through Zone Six, whose inhabitants are Shikastan souls imprisoned there because they have led lives of self-indulgence rather than seeking spiritual growth. Their only chance to escape from Zone Six is to be reborn and relive this stage in their souls' journey. The zones of the title of *Marriages* are presumably those which attract Johor: "I passed many possibilities of slipping over into the other Zones, Zones Four and Five in particular, and, remembering the lively scenes I had observed or taken part in on past visits, it was a real effort to make myself move on" (*Shikasta* 205). These zones are concentric spheres surrounding Shikasta, much like the spheres surrounding the earth in medieval cosmology. However, while the relationship of the souls of Zone Six to Shikasta is explicit, that of the inhabitants of Zones Five, Four, and Three is problematic. Like Shikastans they have corporeal existence, engaging in sexual relations, giving birth, eating (even though some meals are produced by miraculous intervention). Although it may be inferred that the inhabitants of these zones are those who have lived more spiritually aware Shikastan lives than their Zone Six counterparts, such an inference rests on a supposition of cosmographic consistency rather than on textual evidence.

Lessing has said that *Marriages* is "a fable or myth. Also, oddly enough, more realistic."[3] The elements of myth are in the topography of the zones and in the sense of ahistoricity permeating the test—although the flavors of various historical cultures, suitably idealized, are invoked. The care of Zone Three for craftsmanship in both dress and furnishings, for example, is reminiscent of the European fifteenth-century flowering of textiles; and, as Marsha Rowe observes, the military organization of Zone Four bespeaks Imperial Rome, while the tribal organization of Zone Five with its emphasis on communal equality rather than hierarchy suggests the Germanic culture that ultimately overran the Roman Empire.[4] In *Marriages* these different cultural patterns exist concurrently, Zone Four guarding both borders against infiltration by its neighbors. Such a crossbreeding of the cultures is, however, the goal of the Providers, who intend to correct the insularity and concomitant self-satisfaction of Zones Three and Four. The steps they order to correct the sterility of zonal attitudes, symbolized by the increasing infertility of people, animals, and crops, give rise to situations producing reactions clearly recognizable as human emotions, the description of which has always been one of Lessing's strongest abilities. Herein lies both the realism Lessing herself sees in the novel and the main attraction for her readers, amongst whom *Marriages* has been the most popular of the Canopus novels.

*Marriages* continues the exploration of familiar themes: the nature of appropriate parenting; the relations between men and women, humanity and nature, role and personality; the election of the gifted individual; the responsibility of the artist. The one that subsumes all the others, however, continues the dialogue that has occupied Lessing throughout her writing life—the relation of the individual to the collective and of both to a transcendent whole. The novel deals with planned evolution, specifically spiritual evolution, formalizing, as Draine points out, the "stages of consciousness" Lessing has been writing about from the beginning.[5] Using the fabular, mythic relationship of ruler to realm, Lessing deconstructs the relationship between individual and collective, between the personal and the private. She emphasizes that Al·Ith, the queen of Zone Three, and Ben Ata, the king of Zone Four, are not individuals in the way that a citizen of a contemporary republic may be a private individual: "If they were nothing else, these two, they were representatives and embodiments of their respective countries,"[6] a description recalling the correspondences of the medieval Chain of Being, where the microcosm and the macrocosm are not simply analogous but two manifestations of the same idea in the mind of God. For Al·Ith and Ben Ata every act has a significance beyond the actor, with consequences that affect the entire community, as is made clear by the Providers' drum, beating "from that time on, from when they met, until they parted, so that everyone could know they were together, and share in the marriage, in thought, and in sympathetic support— and, of course, in emulation" (69).

The marriage between Al·Ith and Ben Ata, dreaded by both because of the other's alien customs and— worse—alien values, explores a theme appearing in both *Children of Violence* and *The Golden Notebook:* sexual relationships as discovery, extension, evolution of the self. Martha Quest extends her spiritual potential in sexual relationships, particularly with Thomas Stern but also with Jack, a man so sensually gifted that Martha has visionary experiences during the sexual act, and Anna Wulf enters an enlarging and healing breakdown in her relationship with Saul Green, a man who refuses to become imprisoned in either a role or a consistent personality. These three men were all sexually experienced, as was Ben Ata before he married Al·Ith, but, because he has always been in the relation of conqueror to captive, his knowledge of lovemaking is inadequate. In the congress during which Al·Ith becomes pregnant, he is "laid open not only to physical responses he had not imagined, but worse, to emotions he had no desire at all to feel. He was engulfed in tenderness, in passion, in the wildest intensities" (68). For Al·Ith too this submersion in another person is a new experience, although she is a veteran lover and mother of several children. She discovers feelings unknown in Zone Three, such as a "yearning heavy disquiet," when apart from Ben Ata. In Zone Three the emotions are communal matters. As Lusick says, "It is not that we don't feel!—but that feelings are meant always to be directed outwards and used to strengthen a general conception of ourselves and our realm" (5). The ways of Zone Three, stressing cooperation, community, and equality, lead to "peace and plenty"(3), but also, unnoticed by the inhabitants, to stagnation and self-satisfaction. Zone Four, on the other hand, is hierarchical, impoverished by its war machine, its people diminished by a harsh insistence on obedience, particularly that they not "cloud gather," as the inclination to look upward to the glistening mountains of Zone Three is called. In Zone Four men command; women "always give way and never give in" (62), holding festivals of the old songs that keep forbidden knowledge alive. The zone's emphasis on coercion produces negative feelings, as Al·Ith discovers when she is invaded by emotions such as guilt and jealousy, which, unknown in Zone Three, are common in Zone Four. One characteristic, however, the zones have in common. Spiritual growth is as little sought in the freedom of Zone Three as in Zone Four, where looking at the mountains is forbidden. Zone Three has become so complacent, as Al·Ith ruefully understands, that no one thinks of looking up to Zone Two. She herself has not done so since girlhood.

During her marriage to Ben Ata, Al·Ith learns emotions alien to Zone Three that, separating her from the collective, provide the means both for understanding the need for spiritual growth and for attaining it. The spiritual journey she consequently undertakes ultimately benefits the whole community even though it initially causes unrest. When her son Arusi is six months old, the Providers order her back to Zone Three, where she becomes an outcast. Her grief at losing her son and her husband, who must now marry Vahshi of Zone Five, described by Knapp as "a female Genghis Khan,"[7] causes her to be seen as a troublemaker. The changes in attitude she has undergone as a result of her experiences further alienate Zone Three. She is too different, with her sense of enlarged possibilities; the "healthy peaceful faces" of Zone Three now look "fat and mindless" to her (191). Ostracized, Al·Ith becomes an animal tender in the mountains at the foot of the pass to Zone Two. After her visits into the rarefied blueness of Zone Two become known, friends and followers begin to assemble in the neighborhood, with the result that she is put under guard; when Ben Ata comes to see her, he is met at the border by a band armed with catapults, medieval weapons his soldiers find laughable. It seems that even the collective of Zone Three, contented citizens though they are, resent the elect who aspire to higher spiritual regions; feeling threatened when such individuals attract followers equally dissatisfied with an empty existence, they respond in ways that parallel the psychiatric establishment's treatment of Charles Watkins in *Briefing*.

Al·Ith becomes a kind of seer, much in the manner of Lynda Coldridge or Martha Quest. Through repeated visits she gradually grows accustomed to Zone Two "with its crystalline yet liquid substance [holding] her on its surface"—the crystalline substance of the gods' Crystal in *Briefing* and of the state lost souls must strive toward in Zone Six in *Shikasta*. The "barrier [of] the thick clumsy substance of Al·Ith" (196) seems to be gradually burnt away by invisible flames until one day she does not return from Zone Two, whose inhabitants are "like flames, like fire, like light" (230). In increasing numbers others follow her, suggesting that though spiritual growth may be possible for the species, it depends on individual acts of choice. The stages of consciousness do not succeed each other in a straight progression; paradoxically, as Lusick says, "The very high must be matched by the very low . . . and *even fed by it*" (198). Al·Ith clearly learns from the alien emotions of a lower culture, as does the collective of Zone Three, for at the end of the novel migration between the zones is becoming common.

While the events of this novel may slight the claims of individuals, they also suggest that spiritual evolution depends on individual effort because it is in the nature of the collective, no matter how peaceful and prosperous, to maintain the status quo. The static harmony of self and community is not enough; there must be dynamic harmony between communities, which is to be brought about not only by openness of borders and attitudes but also by a general recognition of the need for spiritual evolution. In Lessing's Canopean cosmology there is no Christian separation of body and spirit; the lack of spirituality, the absence of all yearning toward the higher realms, in *Marriages* results in sterility throughout nature. The first step on the path to spiritual evolution, in the unlikely shape of the marriage of Al·Ith and Ben Ata, restores the fertility of both zones. Thus the individual must rise above the personal in the interests of spiritual progress, not for self alone, not for the immediate community, not even for the species, but for the good of animals and plants as well—in short, for the benefit of the transcendent whole.

### *The Sirian Experiments* (1981)

The lesson of *Marriages* is developed at length in *The Sirian Experiments*, where Ambien II's journey to knowledge constitutes the narrative line, just as does Martha Quest's for *Children of Violence*. The education of Ambien, a long-time officer of the Colonial Service, one of the Five who govern the Sirian Empire, takes place over millennia, a slow development made possible by Sirian technology. Because worn body parts are replaced (source unspecified), Sirians are essentially im-

mortal, although they may die by accident or of particularly virulent diseases. Amongst the Five a group mind
prevails to the extent that they know what the others
are thinking or even likely to think. Their common
premises and values seem to be a distillation of the collective mind of all Sirius—if not of the whole empire,
which includes subject species, at least of the mother
planet. Ambien, always "of the liberal party on Sirius"[8]
eventually perceives that the Sirian mind set has *"consistently* led us into wrong judgment" (9). Under the influence of Klorathy, who represents Canopus just as Ambien in this interchange represents Sirius, she begins to
question the premises of the Sirian collective. Sirian culture is pragmatic, technologically astute, progressive,
venturesome, inclined to imperial expansion: as Ambien says, "To *expand* . . . if not normal (in the sense
that it is *right*) is at least the most agreeable position"
(153). In short, it resembles Western culture in certain
important ways.

*Experiments* consists of a report and two appended
letters written by Ambien, who as a first-person narrator should be immediately regarded as unreliable. This
in fact she proves to be; there is always a time lag between her observations and the inferences she draws
from them. Some points she misses entirely. This gap
between what she sees and what readers recognize confers an ironic tension on what would otherwise be an
overly didactic novel. Ambien sets out "to chronicle the
slow, difficult growth of [her] understanding" (270) not

only of the nature of Canopus, which Sirius, interpreting Canopean behavior by projecting its own motivations, had misunderstood, but also of "the Sirian usage of the planet, a new view of ourselves altogether" (215). The report, which covers the same time span as *Shikasta*, is "a new interpretation of history" (8), a "history of the heart rather than of events" (286). Ambien was always a comparatively enlightened administrator, although stupid by Canopean lights because she had no concept of the whole, of the need, the necessity according to which all Canopean activity is judged and to the understanding of which her education under Klorathy's tutelage is directed.

The partiality of Sirius's view of itself is manifest in its inability to foresee the consequences of its own technology, which has rendered the labor of individuals unnecessary, leading to widespread depression and despair, the "existential problem melancholia" (78), familiarly known as "the existentials" (163). This misjudgment transpires because Sirius entertains misconceptions about the fundamental nature of all species: "We had not understood that there is inherent in every creature of this Galaxy a need, an imperative, towards a continual striving, or self-transcendence, or purpose" (14). Ambien sees the problem of the existential affliction as exterior to herself, for although the depression of the displaced workers can not be alleviated by administrative make-work schemes, she herself has meaningful work in colonial administration. The imperative to self-transcendence impels Ambien to seek Canopean enlightenment, which is responsible both for her depression when she understands Sirian limitations, thus becoming marginally aware that her life's work may be meaningless, and for her developing a new role for herself, one function of which is the report that constitutes *The Sirian Experiments*.

Ambien's faith in Sirian rectitude is shaken by the unforeseen outcomes of certain experiments as well as of too-successful technology, of which Sirius has been so proud as to overlook the subtlety of the superior Canopean technology; for example, whereas Sirius extends life by parts replacement, Canopus does so by reincarnation. A Sirian experiment with particularly unsettling results uses the Lombis, a half-ape species, as subjects. They are spacelifted from their own planet to another whose atmosphere compels them to work either in cumbersome space suits or in huge domes under artificial skies. Their work stint done, they are lifted to Rohanda, which they believe is their home planet. Their joyful reactions of wonder and gratitude and their tears disquiet Ambien, who because the usual practice for both Sirius and Canopus is to encourage evolutionary progress, feels she must apologize for the Sirian intention "to keep, just for once, a race on a subservient level" (32). The Lombis interpret their history mythically, ritualizing "their abduction from their home" (30) in monthly ceremonies. In analogy to the workings of Christian grace, they expect to be rescued by celestial strangers who will return them "to their 'real home in the skies'" (30). Here Lessing uses defamiliarization to make her readers rethink traditional versions of history, as she does in numerous other instances in this series.

Evaluating the success of other Sirian experiments in forced evolution, Ambien realizes they have made little real difference in the nature of the species involved, whereas the Canopean pairing of the giants with the indigenous inhabitants of Rohanda has fundamentally changed the native stock. This realization prepares her to learn from Canopus. She perceives that such learning will involve more than intellectual changes. Using the language of such previous Lessing protagonists as Martha Quest and Anna Wulf, she feels that it "may open doors in oneself whose existence one does not do more than suspect" (66); in short, she recognizes her own potential for spiritual growth. This openness to a new kind of experience makes Ambien sensitive to the personality of Klorathy, whom she first meets at an Inter-Empire Conference. They are mutually attracted in a way that promises a sexual encounter with consequent personal growth such as experienced by Al·Ith and Ben Ata, or Anna Wulf and Saul Green; but although Ambien and Klorathy become close over the millennia, their relationship remains that of teacher and student rather than symbiotic lovers. Ambien is always the seeker for knowledge, Klorathy the designer of teaching situations. However, in one instance the influence goes in the other direction. Ambien modifies the way Canopus assigns colonial agents to their posts, but she does this through Nasar, not Klorathy, who remains the instigator of ambiguous experiences, much like Sufi teaching stories, from which she must formulate her own questions and construct her own answers.

These questions all involve purpose: *"who* should use *what* and *how much* and *when* and *what for*?" (81). With "What for?" in her mind, she meets Klorathy on Canopean Planet 11, where the unfamiliar atmosphere, rapid alternation of day and night, and highly evolved insect creatures unnerve her. Here the giants, who have been airlifted from Shikasta, have established a balanced relationship with the indigenous insect race on the basis of *"need"* (105). Ambien keeps running up against the idea of necessity, so foreign to Sirian habits of mind that she has trouble relating it to the Canopean perception of wholeness, unity, harmony. Further, it is some time before she can entertain the idea that a creature looking like "a mass of waving tentacles" (103) might be higher than herself in the evolutionary scale. Her inability to accept Klorathy's explanation that the giants and the insect people "complement each other" (103) indicates that she is resisting both these ideas. She understands that this meeting with Klorathy was intended to teach her something about both Canopus and Sirius, with the underlying expectation that she would, as she eventually does, become "more Canopean than

Sirian" (255), but she sees no direct parallel between herself and Klorathy on the one hand and the giants and the insect people on the other.

Further situations designed by Klorathy for her instruction take place on Shikasta and, because she acts as well as observes, involve her more experientially, a kind of learning valued by Sufis. She understands the nature of evil: "each perfection becomes its opposite" (145). Seeing Nasar fall away from his highest self to the extent that he endangers Ambien, who has been entrusted to his care, she understands that even a Canopean might not be proof against Shammat evil. Though she is herself immune to this kind of temptation—a luxurious decadence of the fleshly pleasures—because, as Nasar says, she is a "dessicated bureaucrat" (131), her personal involvement in the situation enables her to understand. She is, however, susceptible to another kind of temptation, one appropriate to an administrator, when, rescued from imminent sacrifice to Grakconkranpatl (Lessing's defamiliarized Aztec god Quetzacoatl), she refuses to recognize necessity. Seduced into thinking she can avert the inevitable decline of Lelanos, "dwelling on future plans and arrangements" (204), she is captured by the Shammatan Tafta. She understands that, with the connivance of Canopus, she has been led into temptation so that she will protect herself against her susceptibility with the knowledge that "the beginnings of an immersion in evil must always start with something easy, paltry, seemingly unimportant" (210).

Although she fails to do so on the unfamiliar Canopean planet, in another instance she learns by analogic reasoning. Lelannian scientists perform experiments patterned on those conducted by the Nazi Dr. Mengele's operations on Jewish children ostensibly designed to improve surgical techniques. A particularly famous one involved diverting the colon of an eighteen-month-old infant to empty through a stoma above the left hip. In some of the Lelannian operations an extra set of legs is grafted on a child's hips, breasts are transferred to backs, genitalia moved next to mouths. Such experiments force Ambien to reexamine Sirian attitudes toward subject populations, "particularly as regards their use as laboratory material" (234). This reexamination by one who has always advocated policies causing "as little damage to indigenous races as possible" (107) shows the effect of the Canopean lesson on the insidious onset of evil. Considering the variety of creatures in this new world, Lessing seems to be protesting not only race arrogance but species arrogance as well.

This species arrogance, although much modified by her contact with Canopus, still pervades Ambien's thinking. Even though she at last recognizes the superiority of Canopus, she still feels that "it is the duty of the more evolved planets, like the great daughter of Sirius, to guide and control" (235). The prevailing existential melancholia enhances Canopean influence in asking the important questions: if Sirians are driven to debating their nature, the purpose of their existence, they also necessarily have to ask, "What is a genus *for*? . . . What part does it play in the cosmic harmony?" (236). Clearly it does not exist for the express purpose of providing slave labor for another species, a fate Sirius has intended for the Lombis.

Ambien's species loyalty makes her unable to bear what she comes to perceive as the mirage of Sirian greatness, a mirage she has believed in for millennia. "I cannot stand . . . what we are," she tells Klorathy (Lessing's ellipsis), who significantly responds, "But it is not what you will be" (242), hinting, as is the Canopean way, what should be clear enough by now, that Ambien is herself a subject, not a partner, in Canopean forced evolution experiments. In her "role as Sirius" she has interacted with Canopus in a number of stressful environments resulting in such spiritual growth that she now feels "more Canopean than Sirian" (255). Just as the giants interacted with the indigenous species of Rohanda and, after the failure of the Lock, with the insect species of Planet 11, so Canopus has been interacting with Sirius. Ambien is no longer a compatible member of the Five's collective; when she sees their mind as "five globules or cells nestling together in a whole, and one of them pulsing at a different rate" (285), she realizes she has instead become part of a larger "invisible whole" (275). However, there is evidence that, forced into extended leave, which amounts to planet arrest on the significantly numbered Sirian colonised Planet 13, she is not the only beneficiary of the Canopean experiment. Although, as the letter which ends the novel makes clear, she has ostensibly written the report for the Four, she has managed to get it into general circulation in the empire, in every part of which there is now danger of revolution. It appears that the Canopean experiments may have fundamentally changed Sirian nature, as has been the case with their experiments on other species. Ambien's report, in the Canopean way, is ambiguously titled to reflect its double purpose: it records both the Sirian experiments on other species and the Canopean experiments on Sirian subjects, a role for herself that Ambien never quite articulates—rightly, considering her ostensible audience. But in the course of chronicling her own spiritual growth, she suggests the answer to her own question: "What is the purpose of Canopus?" She realizes that Canopus, equally subject to the necessity of the whole, is not the end of the evolutionary chain: "Can it possibly be that just as I watch you, Canopus, while I strive and strive to understand— ... is it possible that just as this is my relation to you, then so is your relation to—to ... (241; Lessing's ellipses). As Sirius is to Canopus in the transcendental scale, so is Canopus to some other beyond her apprehension. Just as Zone One of *Marriages* is beyond both the sight and the imagination of Zone Three, so the next stage in spiritual evolution is beyond the vision of Sirius. Lessing clearly expects her readers, making the parallel analogy, to wonder whether "our view of ourselves as a species on this planet now is inaccurate" (vii).

### *The Making of the Representative for Planet 8* (1982)

This novel provides an extended example of the limits of Canopean power, of Canopus's own subordination to necessity. As Doeg, Memory Maker, the chronicler of the events of the novel, says to Johor, "You are the creation and creatures of something, some Being, to whom you stand in the same relation as we stand to you? some . . . Yes, that must be so"[9]—a comment echoing Ambien II's insight. As in *Shikasta*, where the planetary realignment results in the weakening of the Lock, when climatic changes make Planet 8 no longer hospitable to the species developed through Canopean evolutionary experiments, Johor salvages what he can (in contrast to the Sirian practice of abandoning unprofitable experiments). Like *Marriages, Making* has a fabular component in its descriptions of the Edenic landscape and peaceful communal ways of the inhabitants. The descriptions of weaving and animal husbandry, for example, suggest a fabular medieval time, as does the practice of choosing names according to occupation, much as many European family names—Thatcher,

## *CANOPUS IN ARGOS*

Wainwright, Schumacher, Bouvier—have their origins in medieval custom. Guild sense is strong, each worker feeling an affinity with others performing the same function. These fabular components combined with the paucity of individualizing details necessitate an allegorical reading of *Making*.

The inhabitants of Planet 8 have evolved from four different species, one of which has in its nature an aggressive element encouraging endurance and survival in the face of the advancing ice. Even so, the realization that their future will diverge radically from their expectation brings on an existential despair: "If we are not channels for the future, and if this future is not to be better than we are, better than the present, then what are we?" (39). It is some time before the inhabitants of Planet 8 understand that there will be no next generation at all. Meanwhile they look to Canopus for answers and rescue. When it becomes apparent that Canopus now offers a solution involving new possibilities of spiritual growth for the Representatives and, through them, for the whole population, the subject of the discussion becomes the nature of the individual, the nature of the community, and the relations between them. The prime characteristic of the Representatives of the various functions, elected "to fulfill what we all knew was a general will, a consensus" (42), is their "ordinariness" (54), their typicality: "the 'I' of me is not my own, cannot be, must be a general and shared consciousness" (65). While Doeg intends this to be a statement of the nature of any

Representative on Planet 8, it is particularly appropriate to his function of Memory Maker, thus constituting one more reminder of Lessing's stern notions about the writer's responsibility.

In the interests of achieving through hardship the state of spiritual evolution ensuring salvation, the Representatives try to rouse the population from the despair manifesting as the "deep, dark drive towards sleep, towards death, towards annihilation" (99). They themselves must endure the encroaching ice to the end, outliving the other members of the community so as to gather up all their spiritual essences into a harmonious and transcendental whole: "Their qualities will be reborn. . . . The individual does not matter, the species does not matter" (80). The Representatives struggle to understand the nature of the salvation Canopus now offers. Since their functions are called into being by need, which still exists on other planets, their essence will continue: "Pedug is re-created always and everywhere . . . where Pedug is needed" (108)—one of Lessing's few logistical hints about the nature of the whole. Charged by Canopus with the task of journeying to the freezing Pole, the Representatives, under the guidance of Johor, force themselves forward, much as Al·Ith persisted into Zone Two; however, whereas she is purified by fire, they are purged of corporeal dross by ice. With the eyes of spiritual enlightenment, "a group of individuals, yet a unity" of "feelings, thought, and will" (118), they understand their place in the cosmic dance. Melded into one Representative which includes the essence of Johor, they leave dead Planet 8 and come "to where we are now" (121).

The location of this *where* is nebulous. Considering the advanced state of Canopean technology, which includes not only reincarnation but also the requisitioning of bodies while the owners are still in possession, it may be a repository for transcendental essence, a kind of spiritual zoo or sperm bank. Like the souls in Zone Six awaiting rebirth on Shikasta, the Representative, who does not appear to be on Canopus itself, may perhaps have been reborn on another planet. The identity of *we* is clear enough: although the Representative now is a single entity, it apparently still thinks of itself in the plural. The identity of *you* is more problematic. Although the function of Doeg, Memory Maker, the writer of the chronicle constituting *Making*, is future-oriented, there is no basis in the novel for speculation about who these future beings could be.

Citing her fifty-year fascination with Scott's expeditions in Antarctica in 1901–4 and 1910–13, Lessing's afterword to *Making* gives the source both for the novel's setting and its complex of ideas. Lessing has been forcefully impressed by the way in which members of these expeditions responded to the call to duty, to endurance, even when all hope of survival was gone. The reports of Antarctic cold, which slowed the muscles so severely that getting out of a sleeping bag and into clothes took four hours, are vividly translated into the lethargy of

## UNDERSTANDING DORIS LESSING

Planet 8, though Lessing's own experience of English winters after thirty years in a warm climate perhaps adds an authoritative edge to her persuasive documentation of the effects of cold on body and brain. The descriptions of the encroaching glaciers of the polar landscape are among her most convincing writing.

The emphasis in *Making* on the group's relation to the whole may seem lacking in ordinary concern for the fates of individuals, who after all usually experience aging and dying one by one. However, though such feeling is absent from this novel, it was present in Lessing's consciousness at the time of composition. Just as between *Ripple from the Storm* and *Landlocked* she laid aside *Children of Violence* to write *The Golden Notebook*, so, in a kind of compartmentalization reminiscent of Anna Wulf's fragmentation in *The Golden Notebook*—a similarity enhanced both by Jane Somers's familiar name Janna and the diaries she and Anna keep—Lessing was writing the pseudonymously published *Diaries of Jane Somers*, which focuses on the aging and dying of individuals, at the same time that she was working on *Canopus in Argos*.

### *Documents Relating to the Sentimental Agents in the Volyen Empire* (1983)

This novel takes place on a group of planets outside the Canopean Empire. As in *The Sirian Experiments*, the main narrative line focuses on education, here the education of Incent, a would-be Canopean agent. The record of his many failures and ambiguous successes is provided by Klorathy, his supervisor, whose reports to Johor form the bulk of the novel. Incent is susceptible to Rhetorical Disease, which comes in two main strains. The symptoms of the first are a susceptibility to the emotions roused by words; of the second, a falling into the false categorization of logical operations—an either/or frame of mind antithetical to Lessing's insistence on inclusivity. Both forms of the disease take hold in patients suffering from a congenital weakness, which is the assumption that words can be counted on to reflect reality—"truth," as Lessing calls it. Anna Wulf's discovery of the gap between word and experience contributes to her breakdown; in Incent's case such a perception would constitute a cure. Not only individuals but also empires are threatened by Rhetorical Disease: "a state or empire will be the more long-lived the more its propaganda is not believed in."[10]

The examples of rhetoric Lessing most fiercely satirizes are among the most strongly endorsed by the liberal Western tradition and, not so incidentally, by the protagonists of Lessing's previous novels. The rousing slogans of the French Revolution, the exhortatory speeches from World War Two—including several imitations of Churchill's Dunkirk address—and especially Marxist touchstones all attract her criticism. Variations on such phrases as *the nature of the class struggle, judged at the bar of History*, and *throw off your chains* appear frequently. Once more defamiliarization is at work, asking readers to reevalute their attitudes to events they—and Lessing herself—have felt strongly about. Because in this novel the emphasis is on the type rather than the individual, little identification with the characters is possible. Thus the fullest impact is felt by those who have been themselves involved in the twentieth-century historical events she defamiliarizes.

Readers who have been irked by the invariable rectitude of Canopus will note with some satisfaction that over the series it too has become subject to the cycle of history, to the rise and fall of empire that constitutes one of the major themes of *Agents*. The power of Canopus suffers a setback when, unable to save Planet 8, it is sufficient only for a transcendental blending of essences rather than removal by spaceship; further, all the Canopean agents in this novel, not Incent alone, are susceptible to the rhetorical infections spread by Shammat. Even Klorathy admits to having settled back as "a philosophical spectator of cosmic events, immobilized by the cosmic perspective, . . . addressing the Cosmos itself [with] a sardonic smile on [his] face" (52), which sardonism betrays a susceptibility unthinkable in the Klorathy of *Making*. His overoptimistic prediction of a cure for Incent, with his romantic leanings and his self-selected "large tragic black eyes" (9), is the product of poor judgment, as is perhaps the case with Klorathy's suggestion that reform is possible even for Shammat.

## *CANOPUS IN ARGOS*

*Agents* contains the first suggestions that the impression of Canopean rectitude promulgated so far in the series may in fact be the result of its self-presentation. The corruption of Sirius's expanding empire, which recruits Volyen citizens as spies, invites comparison with Canopus, which also maintains agents in territories belonging to others. A further comparison, this one suggested by Klorathy, also works to Canopean disadvantage: it may be obvious to him that Shammat's statement "we should agree to sink our separate and pitiful little individual wills and thoughts in the great whole, the great Will, the great purpose, the great *Decision*" (61) is a "caricature of Canopus, [a] shabby mimicry" (66); it is not so clear to the reader that this formulation differs much from the Canopean exposition of necessity. His admission that in the past Canopus has made mistakes, has not always worked for "Harmonic Cosmic Development," makes one hope that his view of the emotionless state as the proper one is equally misguided.

The distrust of all institutional propaganda, whether religious, educational, or political, itself undercuts belief in Canopean propaganda (the frequent generalizations about necessity deserve the label). If authority is untrustworthy, why should Canopus be trusted when, articulating its distrust of groups, "the mechanisms that govern us, that make us dance like puppets" (136), it yet advocates the supremacy of the whole, to which all must, of their own choice, their own free will, agree? Why, if words are suspect, are one hundred and fifty books cited as evidence in Grice's lawsuit against Volyen? Why, throughout the novel, are documents presented as reliable sources of information? Further, how can one reconcile Lessing's repeated distrust of words with the position, repeatedly articulated in fiction, essays, and lectures, that the writer is a member of the elect with a special relationship to those who cannot speak for themselves?

In *Canopus* Lessing once more attempts to deconstruct the opposition between the individual and the whole, the outer and the inner, a task she successfully negotiated in the *Children of Violence* through the resonant image of the city, which symbolizes both the inner and the outer state. However, an exploration of polemic and plot (for which the archaic synonym *argument* is useful here) makes this series less compelling. The opposition is tackled through a number of direct explanations, which work less effectively through repetition than does the image of the city, which appears in numerous variations. Lessing continually tries to add points to her argument. Just in case readers have overlooked her meaning, she informs them at the end of *Agents* that submission to the need, the whole, does not imply uniformity or loss of individuality. In its purest form it coexists with happy diversity, appreciation of which paradoxically brings unity: "resting their eyes and their understandings on their own infinite variety, . . .

## *CANOPUS IN ARGOS*

[Volyedestans are] united . . . by their own appreciation of themselves, the richness of their heritage" (176).

Freed though Lessing felt at her discovery of new worlds,[11] their limitations seem to have had a claustrophobic effect. Not only did she break out of *Canopus* to write *The Diaries of Jane Somers*, she also abandoned the series without finishing the sixth novel, already planned and begun, on the grounds that it refused to jell.[12] Her talent seems to lie in the description and analysis of the observed rather than in the creation of the imaginary, as the realistic novels she has written since *Canopus* clearly demonstrate.

## *Notes*

1. Lessing, *Re: Colonised Planet 5, Shikasta* (New York: Knopf, 1979) 40; subsequent references are noted in parentheses.

2. Mona Knapp, *Doris Lessing* (New York: Ungar, 1984) 138.

3. Lessing, preface, *Shikasta* ix.

4. Marsha Rowe, "If you mate a swan and a gander, who will ride?" *Notebooks/Memoirs/Archives*, ed. Jenny Taylor (London: Routledge and Kegan Paul, 1982) 201.

5. Betsy Draine, *Substance under Pressure: Artistic Coherence and Evolving Forms in the Novels of Doris Lessing* (Madison: University of Wisconsin Press, 1983) 162.

6. Lessing, *The Marriages between Zones Three, Four, and Five* (New York: Knopf, 1980) 45; subsequent references are noted in parentheses.

7. Knapp 158.

8. Lessing, *The Sirian Experiments* (New York: Knopf, 1981) 142; subsequent references are noted in parentheses.

9. Lessing, *The Making of the Representative for Planet 8* (New York: Knopf, 1982) 56, Lessing's ellipsis; subsequent references are noted in parentheses.

10. Lessing, *Documents Relating to the Sentimental Agents in the Volyen Empire* (New York: Knopf, 1983) 153; subsequent references are noted in parentheses.

11. Lessing, preface, *Shikasta* ix.

12. Virginia Tiger, "Candid Shot: Lessing in New York City, April 1 and 2, 1984," *Critical Essays on Doris Lessing,* ed. Claire Sprague and Virginia Tiger Boston: Hall, 1986) 222.

# CHAPTER SEVEN

# *The Diaries of Jane Somers* (1984); *The Good Terrorist* 1985); *The Fifth Child (1988)*

Lessing's talent for observation and analysis has never been more clearly demonstrated than in these latest works. Setting aside the cosmic view informing *Canopus in Argos*, here Lessing resumes her interest in the relations between the collective and the individual, specifically the individual unfit for ordinary life. The first-person narrator of *Diaries*, as she herself indicates, is not subject to the "kind of dryness, like a conscience, that monitors Doris Lessing whatever she writes and in whatever style."[1] *Diaries* is characterized by an earnest romanticism—a welcome change from the heavy-handed irony of *Agents*. *The Good Terrorist* and *The Fifth Child* both have an ironic perspective. In spite of the pessimistic view of contemporary Britain *Terrorist* presents, it has a certain comic irony, reminiscent of *Martha Quest*, in the self-aggrandizement of the ne'er-do-wells desperate to be included in the terrorist activities of "the professionals."[2] However, this comic irony turns into tragic irony when their ineptitude leads to a lethal car-bombing. This tragic irony appears in a new permutation in *Child,* where the protagonists are dogged by a malevolent fate more like that permeating the works of Thomas Hardy than *The Grass Is Singing,* where Mary Turner's doom is an inevitable consequence of her character and situation.

### *The Diaries of Jane Somers* (1984)

At the same time that Lessing was writing about a world where "the petty fates of planets, let alone individuals"[3] was insignificant, she was producing under a pseudonym fiction in which the personal anguish missing from *The Making* appears in full measure. *The Diary of a Good Neighbour* and *If the Old Could . . .* (now published together under the title *The Diaries of Jane Somers*) deal in minute detail with the world of individual death and individual responsibility. Considered together, *The Making* and *The Diary* continue the dialogue between the cosmic transcendental perspective and the realistic personal view that has engaged her throughout her work.

In *Diaries* the institutions that have traditionally taken care of the marginal—the family, the welfare state—have proved inadequate. As many, old and young, have been failed by these collectives, new kinds of groups are forming. A number of these are specifically women's communities—a rare kind of collective in Lessing's work—such as the commune where Jane Somers's coworker Hannah lives and the group of eld-

erly women clustered round Eliza Bates who provide
mutual support. The young also look out for each other;
a group of squatters offer to help Jane's niece Kate until
they realize she has been lying to them about the oppression she suffers at Jane's hands.

The internal dialogue in *Diaries* centers on the question of how much the fortunate owe the less fortunate.
Here the concept of privilege, not confined to the inheri-
tors of wealth, extends to those who through their own
efforts have managed to do well in the world. Jane Somers, familiarly known as Janna, has worked since the
age of sixteen, learning her considerable organizational
skills at some cost to herself, as Hannah points out.
Absorbed in her job, she has never paid much attention
to the marginal or the ill, even though her husband and
mother have died of cancer. When Janna befriends
Maudie Fowler, a working-class nonagenarian, her sister implies that such a bizarre friendship is founded on
guilt, although Sister Georgie, who perhaps even more
than Janna will not recognize failure, thinks it perfectly
just that Janna should cope with the inadequately par-
ented Kate.

Janna's relationships with Maudie and Kate make
it clear that nothing one can do, even total immersion
in another life, is enough to stem the rage of the dying
or of the inadequate dependent. Sympathetic as Janna
is, she wonders how Maudie can be so unreasonable as
to be enraged at the prospect of dying at ninety-two.
Maudie suffers from the kind of elderly anger specified

in *The Four-Gated City* as loss of power, here taken to its
ultimate in the loss of life. She does not want social
services to provide a Home Helper or a Good Neighbour, but a particular friend, attached by love not by
duty, even though when Janna does become such a
friend, Maudie cannot contain her resentment. Her
weakening control of her tongue parallels her weakening control of her bladder and bowels; all the resentment she has not dared articulate pours out.

Excessive claims on the attention of another, however, are not confined to the marginal; even the socially
responsible may be unreasonable. Richard, for example,
offers Janna a niche as platonic girlfriend, to take up
which she would have to leave job and country. The
relationships offered Janna all seem unreciprocal, yet
seeing her niece Jill rationing her energies, she winces
as at a repetition of her own mistake. On the other
hand, she clearly thinks her friend and coworker Joyce
has chosen badly in giving up the editorship of *Lilith* to
follow her husband, who has no conception of recipro-
city, to the United States.

In this context in which even the socially privileged
may ask too much, *Diaries* promotes a dialogue about
the way in which societies and individuals concerned
with justice deal with the demand for unconditional
love and continual attention when people have become
marginal because, like Maudie, they are too old to cope
or, like Annie Reeves, have lost touch with ordinary
life, or like Kate, have never attained it or, like John,

### THE DIARIES OF JANE SOMERS

Richard's Down's syndrome son, have been born without any capacity for it. How does the just person manage to balance her own needs—for solitude, for career
growth, for spiritual development—against such
claims? Does one become a Jill, designed for trouble,
Janna thinks, because she does not respond immediately to her lover's demands for affection, or a Kathleen,
so overwhelmed by the injustice of her brother's retar-
dation that she can think of nothing else? Further, how
much can one pay for past lapses? The only person who
seems able to give to an appropriate degree in this grim
stock-taking is Hannah, the maternal lesbian, who,
however, in Janna's judgment falls short because she
opens her arms only to bodies like her own.

*Diaries* is in dialogic relation not only with Canopus
but also with *The Summer before the Dark* and *The Four-
Gated City*. Once more Lessing posits the idea that the
opportunity to play roles refused, whether consciously
or unconsciously, at one time in one's life will reappear
at another. Both these earlier novels deal with the problems of balancing the claims of others against the needs
of one's own development. Janna's life has been the
opposite of Kate Brown's; although she has been married, she has never had children, never played the nurturing role. Like Martha Quest she is presented with a
chance to do so at a later time, so she finds herself
nurturing her teen-age nieces and, as Martha was never
able to do, playing the role of good daughter to an elderly woman becoming increasingly dependent on oth-

ers. *Diaries* suggests that these roles are not, as Kate Brown thinks, necessarily in conflict with real identity; they may, as Martha Quest believes, encourage the development of the inner self provided they are recognized as temporary stages.

The Lessing novel *Diaries* can most profitably be compared with, however, is *The Golden Notebook.* Carey Kaplan points out that Lessing's relation to Jane Somers echoes her relation to Anna Wulf[4]—a suggestion supported by Jane's preferred name, *Janna,* which is paralleled by *Hannah,* just as *Ella* parallels *Anna.* The intertextuality built into the structure of *The Golden Notebook* is replicated in the relations between the *Canopus* novels (especially *The Making*) and *Diaries.* Further, *Diaries* echoes Anna's interest in welfare work manifested in Ella's letter-answering for Dr. West and in the ending of Anna's novel "Free Women," in which her character becomes a social worker.

In addition, *Diaries* contributes to Lessing's prolonged dialogue about the writer's responsibility that constitutes such a prominent concern in *The Golden Notebook.* Janna, a writer as well as an editor of *Lilith,* an upmarket women's magazine, keeps diaries, writes a romantic novel based on Maudie Fowler's reminiscences and articles on the history of fashion for sociological journals. Thus the writer's concern with the act of writing is well represented here. Janna only half articulates her function as representative of those who cannot speak for themselves. She gives voice to the points of view of aged working-class women who clearly cannot command an audience in their own right, taking pains to imagine them completely and sympathetically.

### *The Good Terrorist* (1985)

The tension between its comic and tragic dimensions makes *Terrorist* a vigorous novel different in effect from any of Lessing's previous work. Nonetheless it reworks familiar subjects—leftist politics, the British class structure, the nature of the family, the relations between men and women—in an updated version of the world of *The Golden Notebook*, *The Four-Gated City*, and *The Summer before the Dark*. Alice Mellings's situation resembles Martha Quest's, Kate Brown's, and, to a lesser extent, Anna Wulf's: she is caught up in a woman's complex relation to a house and the concept of home it represents to herself and the other inhabitants. Although she disavows the traditional family, all her efforts are directed toward building a substitute, which provides her sense of self. A daughter of the "rich . . . bourgeoisie" (16) she bargains, manipulates, exploits, and labors to transform a squat into a commune. Thus her situation provides some interesting variations on those of her predecessors.

Anna Wulf, Martha Quest, and Kate Brown, through force of circumstance, character, or intellect, eventually manage to reconcile the claims of biology and history, whereas Alice accommodates neither very well. Her inability to situate herself in her historical moment arises not from any sense of herself as a transcendental being but from some interesting contradictions in her character, contradictions of which she is herself largely unaware. With a naïveté inappropriate to her thirty-six years, she ignores the most obvious questions about herself: Why is she fixated on Jasper, a gay who has leeched off her for fifteen years, stealing her money to finance his orgies? Why does she have incapacitating bouts of rage when confronted by the thought of her father or some other authority figure? Why does she vacillate between anger and protective affection for her mother? Why can't she name the "slicing cold pain" (34) she feels in the presence of a sexually happy couple? Not since Mary Turner has a Lessing novel featured a protagonist so lacking in self-knowledge or desire for spiritual growth.

Her blindness to the dynamics of her own nature is echoed in her relations with others. Although her intuitive understanding helps her choose the functionary most likely to bend the rules when she needs to manipulate the Electricity Board or the Borough Council, she misreads less familiar types with disastrous consequences. Against her conscious will she becomes involved in terrorist activity, and the end of the novel finds her about to be drawn into some unspecified event

## *THE GOOD TERRORIST*

organized by professional terrorists—the IRA, the KGB or their alter ego, MI5.

Alice says proudly, "I am not an intellectual" (247), as though she believes intellectual activity will diminish the intuition on which she sets such store. She reads nothing but newspapers, and even then refuses those from the capitalist press. Although a professed communist, she has read little theory, priding herself on being a home-grown British communist who won't accept directions from outside. For duty she takes care of other like-minded revolutionaries and the odd victim of the Establishment; for pleasure she organizes large meetings, especially parties, for fringe groups like the Communist Centre Union; for excitement she attends demonstrations or, best of all, spray-paints graffiti and runs away from the police. In short, she lives in an emotional present, ignoring any sign of the passing of time, which generally intrudes on her consciousness as change in her mother's circumstances, an irreconcilable quarrel with her oldest friend, for example, or the sale of the family home.

Mrs. Mellings pinpoints the difficulty Alice herself is unable to formulate: "Some people need . . . a long time to grow up"(329). Alice has refused to accept any kind of sexual existence. Even her nesting urge is spurred by a desire to build a family for her own emotional sustenance rather than to nurture a new generation. She does not recognize historical time any more than she acknowledges biological time, revering Lenin, even Trotsky, but never mentioning Mao or Castro. She lives in a kind of allegorical universe that ignores the principle of causality as it operates through time. She refuses to listen to past miseries: "unhappy childhoods are the great con, the great alibi" (121). This opinion is not without justification, but her refusal to understand that acts will have consequences is another matter. She will not accept that if she and Jasper have spent all her mother's money, Mrs. Mellings will have to go without; she does not foresee that if she steals a thousand pounds from her father's business, suspicion will fall on the newest employee. This desire to deny all aspects of time seems to underlie her monstrous rage not merely at the "rich middle class" (13) itself but at middle-class attitudes in general. She is angrier with Mary and Reggie for paying exactly their share of the commune expenses than with Faye, who contributes nothing but spends her Social Security on immediate comforts like whiskey or drugs, or with Jasper, who not only spends his own money on himself but takes hers to finance sado-masochistic homosexual encounters. The key issue is that Mary and Reggie are *savers*, which for Alice is a dirty word, implying a future over which the middle classes expect to exert some control.

The virtues and deficiencies of Alice Mellings's character make her a good vehicle for Lessing's analysis of a segment of the population which, if not increasing, is certainly prominent in Thatcher's Britain. Alice is an acute observer, noticing, for instance, the prevalence of adopted accents, from the refined finishing school to the perky cockney. (The only real cockney in the group is Jim, the black.) Her interpretation of what she sees, however, is untrustworthy, thus allowing a clear view of the ironies and inconsistencies Lessing perceives in this kind of left-wing movement. Few of the would-be-revolutionaries show much concern for those on whose behalf they wish to overthrow the system. Philip and Jim are the only two working-class members of the commune; they want jobs, not revolution. Philip understands that the squatters are exploiting him: "All you people . . . never lift a finger, never do any work, parasites, while people like me keep everything going" (276). When Jim becomes disturbed and disappears, no one but Alice seems to notice. Faye wants to put an end to this "shitty fucking filthy lying cruel hypocritical system . . . so that children don't have a bad time, the way I did" (106), but when a homeless mother with an infant daughter wants a room in the squat, Faye assaults her. The group demands nurturance either from individuals or the state but with few exceptions has no complementary impulse to nurture, wishing only to destroy the system out of some personal need for the aggrandizement or revenge they have valorized into the Cause.

Alice has only a partial understanding of her comrades; her mother seems to be a more trustworthy interpreter. Mrs. Mellings points out the reason for their revolutionary ambitions: the "one thought in your minds, [is] how to get power for yourselves" (334). She offers an explanation: "You've had it so easy all your lives. . . . If you want something, you take it for granted you can have it" (328). Thus Alice's difficulties seem to stem from a privileged childhood rather than a deprived one. In fact, this group seems to be the new leisure class. The "rich middle class" may have property, but it does not have the leisure this commune enjoys, nor the freedom from personal obligations to others. No matter who these revolutionaries think are being taxed for their Social Security, ultimately it is the workers, either in Britain or in the Third World countries where British stockholders invest, who support these leisured laggards.

Lessing's ability to recognize the importance of new character types at the moment of their emergence, one of her greatest gifts, is amply demonstrated in *The Good Terrorist*. Although some of the events in the novel may remind American readers of the 60s, the unrest they arise from is prevalent in British life today, as is the tendency in both Conservative and Labour politicians to seek the answer to current problems in analyses of the past, a form of nostalgia both Anna Wulf of *The Golden Notebook* and Klorathy of *Sentimental Agents* warn against.

## *THE FIFTH CHILD*

### *The Fifth Child* (1988)

This novel stands in dialogic relation to all of Lessing's novels dealing with physical and spiritual evolution, not merely *Canopus in Argos* but also *The Four-Gated City, Briefing for a Descent into Hell, The Summer before the Dark,* and *The Memoirs of a Survivor,* whose nightmare present also contains regressive children. In *The Fifth Child,* Lessing adopts a position radically different from the one producing the children of the future in the appendix to *The Four-Gated City,* who are born higher up the evolutionary scale with extrasensory organs; hypothesizing here a reversion to primitive states of being, she presents the underside of the cosmic view she has struggled so painfully toward.

Like the protagonist of *The Good Terrorist,* the Lovatts in *The Fifth Child* are motivated by drive for family that, unexamined, brings disaster. Both Alice Mellings's and the Lovatts' desires are based on nostalgia, the yearning for a sentimentalized past. Alice Mellings wants to replicate her childhood, David Lovatt to "cancel out all the deficiencies of [his parents'] life."[5] In both novels these similar desires set in motion processes centered on acquiring a house that end in engulfing those who started them. The inevitability of this outcome is recognized too late. Although their lifestyle is very different from that practiced in the terrorist commune, the Lovatts, like Alice, expect their parents to pay, David's

father with his money, Harriet's mother with her labor.
Like Alice they have a poor grip on time, on their historical moment. Also like Alice they have confused role
and identity, seeing their deepest, best selves called into
being by the parental role.

Although the period is clearly specified and contemporary details meticulously described, there is
something fabular, something out of time, about *The
Fifth Child*. The Lovatts cling to a sense of themselves
as "ordinary and in the right of it" (3) in their Victorian
values, but their view is based on a way of life they
have never known. The suddenness with which they
recognize each other as mates suggests a certain fated-
ness in their relationship. Their first lovemaking is conducted with "a deliberate, concentrated intensity" that
indicates David's intention of "taking possession of the
future" (10). Both feel that this occasion is out of ordinary life. Their obsessiveness disturbs Harriet's mother,
who finds their need to "grab everything" ominous. The
extent of their "demand on life" (37) is as excessive as
Alice's, as Maudie Fowler's and Kate's in *Diaries*. A
similar kind of excess marks Harriet's fatalism: she attri-
butes her sister's Down's syndrome daughter to marital
discord, which "probably attracted the mongol child"
(22), while feeling that her own happiness based on
four adorable children is deserved. Hints like this
gradually make it clear that some agency outside ordinary life is driving the plot, just as it did in *The Summer
before the Dark*, for instance, which like *The Fifth Child*

has a realistic surface below which pulls a fabular un-
dertow.

Into the "fortress" (20) the Lovatts have established
against the increasing corruption of the times, reminiscent on a smaller scale of the social breakdown of *Memoirs*, comes a "challenge . . . to destiny" (27), a fifth child
so different he ultimately destroys the family. The difficult pregnancy seems if not the inevitable at least the
foreseeable consequence of the life the Lovatts have
chosen, much like, for instance, the murder of Mary
Turner in *The Grass Is Singing*. The fetus rouses in Harriet thoughts of bizarre experiments reminiscent of the
scientific efforts of Shammat, images of hooves or claws
"cutting her tender inside flesh" (41). Just as Harriet has
blamed Sarah and William for the Down's syndrome
baby, so David begins to blame Harriet. The child is
every bit as alien as they have imagined: his size and
appearance at birth, the bruises he leaves on his
mother's nipples, his attacks on his grandmother and
siblings, his infant habit of throttling family pets earn
him the names of "monster" (47), "troll or goblin" (49),
"Neanderthal" (53), "changeling" (59), "throwback"
(106). David and Harriet feel that he has "willed himself
to be born, [has] invaded their ordinariness" (58),
which, being the product of an intense commitment to
a private vision, is not ordinary at all.

The authorities—the teachers, psychiatrists, and
social workers—will not admit to the fact that Ben is
radically different, not human as the term is generally

understood. They resort to facile explanations, hinting that Harriet simply does not like him enough. The only people who both recognize and accept him are a group of unemployed working-class youths, for whom he becomes a mascot, and his classmates in a secondary modern school, for whom he becomes a leader. (His minimal literacy is clearly a satiric comment on the contemporary British educational system.) When he eventually leaves home with these young thugs, his siblings have scattered, driven away to boarding schools and the homes of relatives, the parents prematurely old, leached of any "metaphysical substance" (112), and thus of any possibility of real identity. Alien genes beyond Harriet's and David's control have wrenched their lives away from their chosen path. They feel that nature has let them down. However, they have too narrow a view of its operations, ignoring its relation to necessity, as Harriet's mother makes clear when she reproaches them for their excesses. When they complain that "having six children, in another part of the world, it would be normal, nothing shocking about it" (16), she points out that in Egypt or India, for example, parents of large families do not expect to raise all their children to adulthood, nor to educate them to live in a technological society. In revering "the processes of Nature" (92), they have slighted history, whose relation to necessity they have chosen to ignore.

Harriet tries to establish a context for what has hap-

pened, mediating between a cosmic evolutionary perspective and an individual personal one. Her perception
that the genes of "all those different people who lived
on earth once—they must be in us somewhere" (114) is
counterbalanced by a sense that she and David are being punished for the hubris of wanting "to be better
than anyone else" (118), the victims of "punishing
Gods, distributing punishments for insubordination"
(118). Her final image of Ben, disappeared into the un-
derworld of some metropolis where he searches for others of his kind, presents him as the harbinger of the
future the Lovatts have tried to ignore.

Clearly Lessing has not yet concluded her career-
long investigation of her major topics. She has probably
not exhausted the subject of evolution, any more than
she has finished with the dialogue between the private
and the public, identity and role, self and other, inner
self and outer self, child and parent, mortality and spirituality, or among the individual, the collective, and the
whole. After writing fiction for forty years, she is still
engaged with the themes and concerns mapped out in
her first novels and stories. Her work may be regarded
as an extended dialogue on the important topics of the
times. In the magnitude of her interests and her dialogic
inclusivity, which makes impossible a final formulation
of her thought, she is a major recorder and interpreter
of the human condition in the twentieth century.

## *Notes*

1. Lessing, preface, *The Diaries of Jane Somers* (New York: Knopf, 1984) 6.

2. Lessing, *The Good Terrorist* (New York: Knopf, 1985) 375; subsequent references are noted in parentheses.

3. Lessing, preface, *Shikasta* (New York: Knopf, 1979) ix.

4. Carey Kaplan, "Britain's Imperialist Past in Doris Lessing's Futurist Fiction," *Doris Lessing: The Alchemy of Survival*, ed. Carey Kaplan and Ellen Cronan Rose (Athens: Ohio University Press, 1988) 156.

5. Lessing, *The Fifth Child* (New York: Knopf, 1988) 13; subsequent references are noted in parentheses.

# BIBLIOGRAPHY

## Works by Lessing
### Novels

*The Grass Is Singing*. London: Michael Joseph, 1950; New York: Crowell, 1950.

*Martha Quest*. Vol. 1 of *Children of Violence*. London: Michael Joseph, 1952; New York: Simon and Schuster, 1964.

*A Proper Marriage*. Vol. 2 of *Children of Violence*. London: Michael Joseph, 1954; New York: Simon and Schuster, 1962.

*Retreat to Innocence*. London: Michael Joseph, 1956.

*A Ripple from the Storm*. Vol. 3 of *Children of Violence*. London: Michael Joseph, 1958; New York: Simon and Schuster, 1966.

*The Golden Notebook*. London: Michael Joseph, 1962; New York: Simon and Schuster, 1962.

*Landlocked*. Vol. 4 of *Children of Violence*. London: MacGibbon and Kee, 1965; New York: Simon and Schuster, 1966 (vols. 3 and 4 published in a single book).

*The Four-Gated City*. Vol. 5 of *Children of Violence*. London: MacGibbon and Kee, 1969; New York: Knopf, 1969.

*Briefing for a Descent into Hell*. London: Jonathan Cape, 1971; New York: Knopf, 1975.

*The Summer before the Dark*. London: Jonathan Cape, 1973; New York: Knopf, 1973.

*The Memoirs of a Survivor*. London: Octagon Press, 1974; New York: Knopf, 1975.

*Re: Colonised Planet 5, Shikasta*. Vol. 1 of *Canopus in Argos: Archives*. London: Jonathan Cape, 1979; New York: Knopf, 1979.

*The Marriages Between Zones Three, Four, and Five*. Vol. 2 of *Canopus in Argos: Archives*. London: Jonathan Cape, 1980; New York: Knopf, 1980.

*The Sirian Experiments*. Vol. 3 of *Canopus in Argos: Archives*. London: Jonathan Cape, 1981; New York: Knopf, 1981.

*The Making of the Representative for Planet 8*. Vol. 4 of *Canopus*

### BIBLIOGRAPHY

*in Argos: Archives*. London: Jonathan Cape, 1982; New York: Knopf, 1982.

*Documents Relating to the Sentimental Agents in the Volyen Empire*. Vol. 5 of *Canopus in Argos: Archives*. London: Jonathan Cape, 1983, New York: Knopf, 1983.

*The Diaries of Jane Somers*. New York: Knopf, 1984. Originally published in two volumes as *The Diary of a Good Neighbour* and *If the Old Could . . . by Jane Somers* (London: Michael Joseph, 1983–84; New York: Knopf, 1983–84).

*The Good Terrorist*. London: Jonathan Cape, 1985; New York: Knopf, 1985.

*The Fifth Child*. London: Jonathan Cape, 1988; New York: Knopf, 1988.

**Short Novels and Short Stories**

*This Was the Old Chief's Country*. London: Michael Joseph, 1951; New York: Crowell, 1952. Short Stories.

*Five: Short Novels*. London: Michael Joseph, 1953.

*The Habit of Loving*. London: MacGibbon and Kee, 1957. New York: Crowell, 1957. Short Stories.

*A Man and Two Women*. London: MacGibbon and Kee, 1963. New York: Simon and Schuster, 1963. Short Stories.

*African Stories*. London: Michael Joseph, 1964; New York: Simon and Schuster, 1965.

*The Temptation of Jack Orkney*. London: Jonathan Cape, 1972; New York: Knopf, 1972. Short Stories.

*Stories*. New York: Knopf, 1978.

**Autobiography**

*Going Home*. London: Michael Joseph, 1957; New York: Ballantine, 1968.

*In Pursuit of the English: A Documentary*. London: MacGibbon and Kee, 1960; New York: Simon and Schuster, 1961.

## BIBLIOGRAPHY

*Particularly Cats*. London: Michael Joseph, 1967; New York: Simon and Schuster, 1967.

"My Father." *Sunday Telegraph*, 1 Sept. 1963. Rpt. *A Small Personal Voice*, ed. Paul Schlueter. New York: Knopf, 1974. 83–86.

"Impertinent Daughters." *Granta* 14 (Winter 1984):51–68.

"Autobiography (Part Two): My Mother's Life." *Granta* 17 (Autumn 1985):225–38.

**Essays**

"The Small Personal Voice." *Declaration*, ed. Tom Maschler. London: MacGibbon and Kee, 1957. Rpt. *A Small Personal Voice*, ed. Schlueter. 3–21.

"An Ancient Way to New Freedom." *Vogue* 15 Dec. 1971. 98, 125, 130–31. Rpt. *The Diffusion of Sufi Ideas in the West*, ed. Leonard Lewin. Boulder: Keysign Press, 1972; and *The Elephant in the Dark and Other Writings on the Diffusion of Sufi Ideas in the West*, ed. Leonard Lewin. New York: Dutton, 1976. 73–81.

"In the World, Not of It." *Encounter* 39 (Aug. 1972):61–64. Rpt. *A Small Personal Voice*, ed. Schlueter. 129–39.

"On *The Golden Notebook*." *Partisan Review* 40 (Winter 1973):14–30. Rpt. *A Small Personal Voice*, ed. Schlueter. 23–45. Has appeared as the introduction to editions of *The Golden Notebook* since 1972.

*Prisons We Choose to Live Inside*. London: Picador, 1987; New York: Harper, 1987.

*The Wind Blows Away Our Words*. London: Picador, 1987; New York: Vintage, 1987.

**Anthology**

*The Doris Lessing Reader*. London: Jonathan Cape, 1988; New York: Knopf, 1988. Short stories, novel excerpts, nonfiction.

## BIBLIOGRAPHY

**Plays**

*Each His Own Wilderness. New English Dramatists, Three Plays*, ed. E. Martin Browne. Harmondsworth: Penguin, 1959.

*Play with a Tiger: A Play in Three Acts.* London: Michael Joseph, 1962. Rpt. *Plays by and about Women*, ed. Victoria Sullivan and James Hatch. New York: Random House, 1973. 201–75.

**Poetry**

*Fourteen Poems.* Northwood, Middlesex: Scorpion Press, 1959.

## Critical Works
**Interviews**

Bannon, B. A. "Authors and Editors." *Publishers Weekly* 2 June 1969: 51–54.

Bergonzi, Bernard. "In Pursuit of Doris Lessing." *New York Review of Books* 11 Feb. 1965: 12–14.

Bertelsen, Eve. "An Interview with Doris Lessing." *Journal of Commonwealth Literature* 21 (1986): 134–61.

Bigsby, C. W. E. "Doris Lessing: An Interview." *The Radical Imagination and the Liberal Tradition.* London: Junction Press, 1981. 188–208.

Bikman, Minda. "A Talk with Doris Lessing." *New York Times Book Review* 30 Mar. 1980: 24–27.

Braudeau, Michel. "Doris Lessing: du marxisme au soufisme." *L'Express* 5 May 1981: 96–103.

Driver, C. J. "Profile 8: Doris Lessing." *New Review* 8 (Nov. 1974): 17–23.

Hazelton, Lesley. "Doris Lessing on Feminism, Communism and Space Fiction." *New York Times Magazine* 25 July 1982: 20+.

Howe, Florence. "A Conversation with Doris Lessing." *Con-*

## BIBLIOGRAPHY

*temporary Literature* 14 (Autumn 1973): 418–36. Rpt. *A Small Personal Voice*, ed. Schlueter. 77–82.

Langley, Lee. "Scenarios of Hell." London *Guardian Weekly* 24 Apr. 1971: 14.

Newquist, Roy. "Interview with Doris Lessing" *Counterpoint*. Rand McNally, 1964, 413–24. Rpt. *A Small Personal Voice*, ed. Schlueter. 45–60.

Oates, Joyce Carol. "A Visit with Doris Lessing." *Southern Review* 9 (Autumn 1973): 873–83.

Raskin, Jonah. "Doris Lessing at Stony Brook: An Interview." *New American Review 8*. New York: New American Library, 1970. 166–79. Rpt. *A Small Personal Voice*, ed. Schlueter. 61–76.

Rihiot, Catherine. "Doris Lessing: An Interview." *F Magazine* June 1981: 41 + .

Torrents, Nissa. "Doris Lessing: Testament to Mysticism." Trans. Paul Schlueter. *Doris Lessing Newsletter* 4.2 (Winter 1980): 1 + .

**Bibliography**

Seligman, Dee. *Doris Lessing: An Annotated Bibliography of Criticism*. Westport, CT: Greenwood Press, 1981.

**Books**

Bloom, Harold, ed. *Doris Lessing*. New York: Chelsea House, 1986. This collection of some of the better-known articles on the fiction, because it is organized chronologically, serves as a history of changing attitudes in Lessing criticism. The editor's introduction is both patronizing and eccentric.

Brewster, Dorothy. *Doris Lessing*. New York: Twayne, 1965. This first book-length study of the fiction is of limited usefulness because it covers no work later than *Landlocked*.

# BIBLIOGRAPHY

Budhos, Shirley. *The Theme of Enclosure in Selected Works by Doris Lessing*. Troy, NY: Whitston, 1987. Examines the theme of enclosure, particularly as manifested in marriage, in selected texts.

Draine, Betsy. *Substance under Pressure: Artistic Coherence and Evolving Forms in the Novels of Doris Lessing*. Madison: University of Wisconsin Press, 1983. Hypothesizes that Lessing's dialectical formal development explains the varied surfaces of her novels while her basic themes have remained unchanged.

Fishburn, Katherine. *The Unexpected Universe of Doris Lessing*. Westport, CT: Greenwood Press, 1985. Demonstrates the techniques by which the space fiction teaches new ways of looking at the world.

Kaplan, Carey, and Ellen Cronan Rose, eds. *Doris Lessing: The Alchemy of Survival*. Athens: Ohio University Press, 1988. Previously unpublished articles.

————. *Approaches to Teaching Lessing's* The Golden Notebook. New York: Modern Language Association, 1989. The articles solicited for this volume provide specific historical, political, and philosophical information and suggest teaching strategies to make the novel more accessible.

Knapp, Mona. *Doris Lessing*. New York: Ungar, 1984. General introduction, including a useful chronology, which covers the complete works through *Canopus in Argos*.

Pratt, Annis, and L. S. Dembro, eds. *Doris Lessing: Critical Studies*. Madison, University of Wisconsin, 1974. Rpt. of special issue on Lessing by *Contemporary Literature*, Autumn 1973.

Rose, Ellen Cronan. *The Tree Outside the Window: Doris*

## BIBLIOGRAPHY

*Lessing's "Children of Violence."* Hanover, NH: University Press of New England, 1976. Uses Erik Erikson's theory of ego development to analyze the psychological growth of Martha Quest.

Rubenstein, Roberta. *The Novelistic Vision of Doris Lessing: Breaking the Forms of Consciousness.* Urbana: University of Illinois Press, 1979. Covering the novels through *Memoirs*, this book perceives the common denominator of Lessing's work as the evolution of the conscious mind, which is characterized by the tension between analytical and symbolic thought.

Sage, Lorna. *Doris Lessing.* New York: Methuen, 1983. This monograph, dealing with the novels through *Making*, considers Lessing's colonial experience as central to her identity as a writer.

Schlueter, Paul, ed. *The Fiction of Doris Lessing.* Evansville: University of Evansville Press, 1971. Previously unpublished articles.

———. *The Novels of Doris Lessing.* Carbondale: Southern Illinois University Press, 1969. One of the earliest works on Lessing, discussing the novels through *Briefing*.

———. *A Small Personal Voice.* New York: Knopf, 1974. Collected interviews and essays by Lessing.

Singleton, Mary Ann. *The City and the Veld: The Fiction of Doris Lessing.* Lewisburg, PA: Bucknell University Press, 1977. Analyzes the imagery of the integration of consciousness with the unconscious in the novels through *Memoirs*.

Sprague, Claire. *Rereading Doris Lessing.* Chapel Hill: University of North Carolina Press, 1987. Subtitled "Narrative Patterns of Doubling and Repetition," this book discovers sub-

# BIBLIOGRAPHY

versive meanings below the surface of selected Lessing novels. Especially useful chapter on *Retreat to Innocence*, a novel that has so far received little commentary.

———. *In Pursuit of Doris Lessing: Nine Nations Reading*. London: Macmillan, 1990. Collection of essays examining a Lessing who remains as international and transcultural as she is African and English.

———. and Virginia Tiger, eds. *Critical Essays on Doris Lessing*. Boston: Hall, 1986. Collection of articles and reviews, some previously unpublished; an excellent introduction succinctly outlines Lessing's career to date and gives an overview of major positions in Lessing criticism.

Taylor, Jenny, ed. *Notebooks/Memoirs/Archives: Reading and Re-reading Doris Lessing*. London: Routledge and Kegan Paul, 1982. This collection of essays by women living in Britain suggests that British readings of Lessing are more likely than American readings to be situated in a political rather than a psychological or formal context.

Thorpe, Michael. *Doris Lessing's Africa*. London: Evans Brothers, 1978. Maintains that Lessing is essentially an African writer and suggests that her preferred situation in relation to her material is that of outsider.

Whittaker, Ruth. *Doris Lessing*. New York: St. Martin's, 1988. A general overview of the fiction through *The Good Terrorist*.

**Special Journal Issues**

*Contemporary Literature* 14 (Autumn 1973), ed. Annis Pratt and L. S. Dembo.

*Modern Fiction Studies* 26 (Spring 1980), ed. Margaret Church and William T. Stafford.

**Newsletter**

*The Doris Lessing Newsletter*. The Doris Lessing Society (1976– ).

# BIBLIOGRAPHY

## Selected Articles

Allen, Orphia Jane. "Structure and Motif in Doris Lessing's *A Man and Two Women*." *Modern Fiction Studies* 26 (Spring 1980):63–74. Treating the short story collection *A Man and Two Women* as a coherent structure, this article examines the relationship between the self and the collective.

Bertelsen, Eve. "Who Is It Who Says 'I'?: The Persona of a Doris Lessing Interview." *Doris Lessing: The Alchemy of Survival*, ed. Kaplan and Rose. 169–82. This extraordinarily interesting article attempts to "discover the terms of the discourse" of a Lessing interview, which turn out to "constitute a code of authorial control."

Carey, John L. "Art and Reality in *The Golden Notebook*." *Contemporary Literature* 14 (Autumn 1973):437–57. Rpt. *Doris Lessing: Critical Studies*, ed. Pratt and Dembo. 20–40. An excellent article arguing that the structure of *The Golden Notebook* illustrates the inseparability of art and life.

Chaffee, Patricia. "Spatial Patterns and Closed Groups in Lessing's *African Stories*." *South Atlantic Bulletin* 43 (1978):42–52. One of the few about Lessing's African fiction, this article suggests that the conflicts between insiders and outsiders are manifested in terms of physical and psychological boundaries.

Drabble, Margaret. "Doris Lessing: Cassandra in a World under Siege." *Ramparts* 10 (Feb. 1972):50–54. Rpt. *Critical Essays on Doris Lessing*, ed. Sprague and Tiger. 183–91. Gives an accurate picture of how Lessing's work through *The Golden Notebook* and *The Four-Gated City* appeared to perceptive readers.

Fishburn, Katherine. "Wor(l)ds Within Words: Doris Lessing as Meta-Fictionist and Metaphysician." *Studies in the Novel*

## BIBLIOGRAPHY

20 (Summer 1988):186–205. Argues that Lessing, never truly the realist she appeared to be, has always leaned toward metafictionality in her attempts to expose the falsity of prevalent conceptions of reality.

Hanson, Clare. "The Woman Writer as Exile: Gender and Possession in the African Stories of Doris Lessing." *Critical Essays on Doris Lessing,* ed. Sprague and Tiger. 107–14. Using Lessing's own categories of masculine and feminine prose styles as exemplified in "The Pig" and "The Trinket Box," this article suggests the possibility of a relationship between Lessing's masculine style and the theme of colonization.

Hardin, Nancy Shields. "Doris Lessing and the Sufi Way." *Contemporary Literature* 14 (Autumn 1973):565–82. Rpt. *Doris Lessing: Critical Studies,* ed. Pratt and Dembo. Analyzes the part that Sufism, which attempts to expand the individual consciousness to include the nonrational, plays in the development of Lessing's thought.

———. "The Sufi Teaching Story and Doris Lessing." *Twentieth Century Literature* 23 (1977):314–25. Rpt. *Doris Lessing: Critical Studies.* 121–32. Explains the nature and function of Sufi teaching stories which, open-ended, elicit a variety of interpretations with a view to modifying the thinking process itself.

Hynes, Joseph. "The Construction of *The Golden Notebook.*" *Iowa Review* 4 (1973):100–13. Presents an excellent analysis of the structure of *The Golden Notebook,* defining the author of the various parts and explaining how they fit together.

Jong, Erica. "Everywoman out of Love?" *Partisan Review* 40 (1973):500–503. Rpt. *Critical Essays on Doris Lessing,* ed. Sprague and Tiger. 197–99. This review of *The Summer before the Dark* points out that although the novel purports to be

**BIBLIOGRAPHY**

about the problems of Everywoman, her existential dilemma is everyone's.

Kaplan, Carey. "Britain's Imperialist Past in Doris Lessing's Futurist Fiction." *Doris Lessing: The Alchemy of Survival*, ed. Kaplan and Rose. 149–58. Suggests that *Canopus in Argos* is essentially autobiographical, consisting of depersonalized chronicles of the aging process that recommend "resignation and insistence on a long view."

Krouse, Agate Nesaule. "Doris Lessing's Feminist Plays." *World Literature Written in English* 15 (1976):305–22. A useful article comparing *Play with a Tiger* to *The Golden Notebook* and analyzing the problems of maternal responsibility presented in *Each His Own Wilderness*.

Magie, Michael L. "Doris Lessing and Romanticism." *College English* 38 (1977):531–52. This important article rejects a major Lessing premise, criticizing as self-indulgent her approbation of irrationalism, mysticism, and madness as paths to enlightenment.

Marchino, Lois. "The Search for Self in the Novels of Doris Lessing." *Studies in the Novel* 4 (1972):252–61. Discusses *The Golden Notebook, The Four-Gated City,* and *Briefing for a Descent into Hell* as searches for self in a world of alienated heroines.

Markow, Alice Bradley. "The Pathology of Feminine Failure in the Fiction of Doris Lessing." *Critique* 16 (1974):88–100. Analyzes women characters from *The Grass Is Singing* through *The Summer before the Dark,* concluding that Lessing is urging women to shun dependency and to assume responsibility for a self.

Mulkeen, Anne M. "Twentieth-Century Realism: The 'Grid' Structure of *The Golden Notebook.*" *Studies in the Novel* 4

## BIBLIOGRAPHY

(1972):262–74. Describes *The Golden Notebook* as the "criss-crossing" of a multiplicity of viewpoints with a multiplicity of events.

Pickering, Jean. "Marxism and Madness: The Two Faces of Doris Lessing's Myth." *Modern Fiction Studies* 26 (Spring 1980):17–30. Argues that there is no essential conflict between Lessing's "politics of the left" and her "politics of madness" as they are both manifestations of the image of the ideal city that structures her world view.

Porter, Dennis. "Realism and Failure in *The Golden Notebook*." *Modern Language Quarterly* 35 (1974):56–65. Discusses the role of realism in *The Golden Notebook*, which Lessing uses against itself to reveal its inability to tell the truth.

Porter, Nancy. "Silenced History—*Children of Violence* and *The Golden Notebook*." *World Literature Written in English* 12 (1973):161–79. Points out that, by recording the histories of the displaced, Lessing gives voice to the silenced. Includes a discussion of time in *The Golden Notebook*.

Rapping, Elayne Antler. "Unfree Women: Feminism in Doris Lessing's Novels." *Women's Studies* 3 (1975):29–44. Describes Lessing's movement away from individualistic feminism in *The Golden Notebook* toward a collective feminine consciousness in *The Four-Gated City*.

Rose, Ellen Cronan. "Doris Lessing's *Città Felice*." *Massachusetts Review* 24 (Summer 1983):369–86. Rpt. *Critical Essays on Doris Lessing*, ed. Sprague and Tiger. 141–53. Argues that relating Martha's ideal city to the *città felice* of Renaissance Italian architecture as well as to Jungian and Sufi thought illuminates the path by which Lessing moved from *Martha Quest* to *Canopus*.

Rowe, Marsha. "If you mate a swan and a gander, who will

## BIBLIOGRAPHY

ride?" *Notebooks/Memoirs/Archives*, ed. Jenny Taylor. 191–205. Considers the implications of analyzing *Marriages* through a series of different interpretive strategies.

Seligman, Dee. "The Sufi Quest." *World Literature Written in English* 12 (1973): 190–206. Argues that Sufism explains Thomas Stern's role in expanding Martha's consciousness and provides the key for integrating the appendix with the body of *The Four-Gated City*.

———. "The Four-Faced Novelist." *Modern Fiction Studies* 26 (Spring 1980):3–16. Describes the author's meeting with various people in Rhodesia, Harry Tayler among them, who knew Lessing before she emigrated to England.

Stimpson, Catharine. "Doris Lessing and the Parables of Growth." *The Voyage In: Fictions of Female Development*, ed. Elizabeth Abel, Marianne Hirsch, and Elizabeth Langland. Hanover, N: University Press of New England, 1983. 176–90. Rpt. *Doris Lessing*, ed. Bloom. 183–200. An intelligent synthesis of the best that has been thought and said about *Children of Violence*, providing an overall look at Lessing's exposition of woman's potential for psychological growth.

Stitzel, Judith. "Reading Doris Lessing." *College English* 40 (1979):498–504. Answers Magie's charges, arguing that reason consists of taking account of all kinds of experience, even the paradoxical.

Sullivan, Alvin. *"The Memoirs of a Survivor:* Lessing's Notes toward a Supreme Fiction." *Modern Fiction Studies* 26 (Spring 1980):157–62. Argues that the meaning of *Memoirs* lies in the reader's establishing connections in the process of reading.

Taylor, Jenny. "Memory and Desire on Going Home: The Deconstruction of a Colonial Radical." *Critical Essays on Doris Lessing*, ed. Sprague and Tiger. 37–44. Analyzes the com-

# BIBLIOGRAPHY

plexities of *Going Home* as a colonial text, examining the relations between documentary, fiction, and autobiography.

Tiger, Virginia. "Candid Shot: Lessing in New York City, April 1 and 2, 1984." *Doris Lessing Newsletter* 8 (Fall 1984):5–6. Rpt. *Critical Essays on Doris Lessing*, ed. Sprague and Tiger. 221–23. This report includes lengthy quotations from Lessing's remarks, most prominently a description of the evolution of *Marriages*.

Vlastos, Marion. "Doris Lessing and R. D. Laing: Psychopolitics and Prophecy." *PMLA* 91 (Mar. 1976):245–58. Rpt. *Critical Essays on Doris Lessing*, ed. Sprague and Tiger. 126–41. Analyzes *The Golden Notebook*, *The Four-Gated City*, and *Briefing for a Descent into Hell* according to the tenets of R. D. Laing.

Zak, Michele W. *"The Grass Is Singing:* A Little Novel About the Emotions." *Contemporary Literature* 14 (Autumn 1973):481–90. Rpt. *Doris Lessing: Critical Studies*, ed. Pratt and Dembo. Argues that *Grass* is structured by the dialectical relationship between the circumstances of the individual life and the material nature of the social and economic system.

# INDEX

# INDEX

# INDEX

## INDEX

## INDEX

# INDEX

## INDEX

## INDEX

## INDEX

## INDEX

## INDEX

## INDEX

# INDEX